A Prophet's Last Words

A Prophet's Last Words

GUNNAR MILTON JOHNSON

Unity Publishers
A Division of Synergy Publishing
Alachua, Florida 32615

Unity Publishers
A Division of Synergy Publishing
Alachua, Florida 32615

A Prophet's Last Words
by Gunnar Milton Johnson

Copyright © 2007 by Zelma Johnson

Printed in the United States of America.

Library of Congress Catalog Card Number: 2007940840
International Standard Book Number 978-1-931-727-21-1

Scripture quotations are from the *King James Version* of the Bible.

Dedication

Dedicated to the body of Christ

and the prophetic voices that are yet to come.

Introduction

In a world of ever shifting seasons, the prophetic word, married with Scripture, brings life with a solid foundation. These words inspire, encourage, correct, edify and confirm what God is speaking to His people today.

As the Beloved of the Lord, we have many questions and struggles. We want to grow in our spiritual giftings, and continue to hear God accurately. We long for an intimate connection with the Heavenly Father, and yet we struggle to overcome discouragement as we move through this earthly life. As His truth speaks into our spirit and soul, we pray these words will personally bring forth truth and life for you.

Pastor Gunnar Milton Johnson, a Lutheran pastor, came through the Charismatic Movement of the 1970s. He began moving in the prophetic gifting as he fully embraced the Holy Spirit. After an intense battle with the enemy, he was encouraged to write the Psalms. This writing became a part of him and grew into the prophetic words he received from the Lord. He immersed himself in Scripture and prayer and was led to pastor a small, nondenominational, charismatic fellowship. This gave him the opportunity to fully focus on God, prayer, Scripture and writing. The prophetic words he received were shared by thousands around the world.

In August 2002, Pastor Gunnar Milton Johnson went home to the Lord. A great many recipients of his words immediately felt the loss. After a time, we began to gather together some of the last words he had received. Some of these last words were not previously shared with his subscribers until now. The dates that the words were received as well as some locations are noted.

These words are timeless. We encourage you to absorb them slowly with the Scripture. Allow God to speak deep into you.

May God bless you as you read.

Word Received February 24, 2002

My eagles will come screaming as they soar before the Ancient of Days in worship and celebration. The cloud of my glory will cover you with my righteousness and joy. I am lifting you up from the darkness that has tried to discourage you. I am partnering you with those I have chosen for the great crusade that I am launching upon the earth. My followers will be filled with a fresh enthusiasm and zeal for my Kingdom. I am joining you together in a bond that cannot be broken for it is anointed by my love. I am drawing aside the curtain so you will catch a glimpse of what I will be doing in these last days. My trumpets are calling my people to attention to hear the marching orders that I have for them. You are also being singled out for my purposes in this time. Listen attentively to my Holy Spirit as he stirs within you. He is releasing the fire you will need to carry you through to the final goal I have set for you. It is a cleansing fire, which will drive out the impurities that have stubbornly remained in you. It will be a fire of inspiration, which will release a fresh creativity in you. All of this is for the reestablishing of my rule among you. The host of heaven will join you in the final preparations for my coming again. They will do battle in the places you cannot go. The final strongholds of the enemy will be vanquished. Hearts and minds that have been held captive by the lies of the enemy will be set free. My truth will come pouring out upon you and my light will burst forth in you. My love will accomplish mighty works for my Kingdom as it takes hold of your total being. My Spirit will lead you into the places I have prepared for you. Set the sails of your heart to catch the wind of my Spirit as it begins to blow with a new intensity. My will for you is perfect and it will be accomplished!

Love,
JESUS

1

Revelation 15

¹Then I saw another sign in heaven, great and marvelous: seven angels having the seven last plagues, for in them the wrath of God is complete.

²And I saw something like a sea of glass mingled with fire, and those who have the victory over the beast, over his image and over his mark and over the number of his name, standing on the sea of glass, having harps of God. ³And they sing the song of Moses, the servant of God, and the song of the Lamb, saying: "Great and marvelous are Your works, Lord God Almighty! Just and true are Your ways, O King of the saints! ⁴Who shall not fear You, O Lord, and glorify Your name? For You alone are holy. For all nations shall come and worship before You, for Your judgments have been manifested." ⁵After these things I looked, and behold, the temple of the tabernacle of the testimony in heaven was opened. ⁶And out of the temple came the seven angels having the seven plagues, clothed in pure bright linen, and having their chests girded with golden bands. ⁷Then one of the four living creatures gave to the seven angels seven golden bowls full of the wrath of God who lives forever and ever. ⁸The temple was filled with smoke from the glory of God and from His power, and no one was able to enter the temple till the seven plagues of the seven angels were completed.

Word Received February 25, 2002

My presence goes with you wherever you go and in whatever circumstance you find yourself. Trust my Spirit as he has taken charge of your life! He is the one who knows me best and who knows you best as well. He has joined us together for the purposes of my Kingdom and he will carry out my plans in your life. Proceed in what he gives you and refrain from those things that are not your concern for I will deal with them! Enjoy my working in you and live with great expectations for what the future will bring. I will lay it all out before you when the time is ripe. Continue to seek my face as you worship the Righteous Father in a true spirit of humility and devotion! All things will come together at the appointed time. I am building up my people to be a royal priesthood of holy intercessors and servants in my sanctuaries. What may seem impossible to the natural eye will have great possibilities in my hands. I am gathering my beloved ones into a fellowship of divine proportions which no one can prevail against in their greatest challenges. The darkness will quickly dissipate before the light of my truth. The thoughts of man will grow strangely dim as they encounter the glory of my righteousness. Even the most lost soul can be transformed as they come face to face with the reality of who I am. Peace and joy surround me and they are imparted to all who receive me for who I am. Your prayers avail much even when they seem to go nowhere in your estimation. They are carried on angel's wings until they are implemented according to my intentions. My Spirit is alive and active in them for they are my grace being poured out on the earth. Your place is in the middle of them and you cannot always see their outcome until later. Continue to lift up those I place before you by my Spirit as a faithful servant!

Love,

JESUS

James 5:13-18

¹³Is anyone among you suffering? Let him pray. Is anyone cheerful? Let him sing psalms. ¹⁴Is anyone among you sick? Let him call for the elders of the church, and let them pray over him, anointing him with oil in the name of the Lord. ¹⁵And the prayer of faith will save the sick, and the Lord will raise him up. And if he has committed sins, he will be forgiven. ¹⁶Confess your trespasses to one another, and pray for one another, that you may be healed. The effective, fervent prayer of a righteous man avails much. ¹⁷Elijah was a man with a nature like ours, and he prayed earnestly that it would not rain; and it did not rain on the land for three years and six months. ¹⁸And he prayed again, and the heaven gave rain, and the earth produced its fruit.

Word Received February 26, 2002

The light of my glory is about to explode in your midst. It will transform you as nothing else can. All that you have been waiting for will quickly surface among you. My ways will truly become your ways as you pursue the fulfillment of my Kingdom. My sovereignty will become more and more apparent as you yield to my Holy Spirit and allow him full sway in your lives. I have been building your life in me piece-by-piece and moment-by-moment. You are approaching the pinnacle of the mountain even though you cannot clearly see it. Still trust my wisdom and my grace in everything that is taking place! There will be clouds but my sunshine will always break through ultimately. I have sown the seeds in the lives that have been dedicated to me. I only needed small openings and a quick moment to accomplish it. The roots have been going deep especially in the dry times, but when the latter rain of my Spirit begins to fall there will be a great harvest. Showers of blessings will accompany all that I will be doing in your life. I appreciate you even if no one else does. You are precious in my sight and the Righteous Father rejoices over you with singing. The days ahead will become more prosperous for you in the timing of my Kingdom. I will satisfy your needs in ways you never even considered. I will do it abundantly. Continuously seek my face in worship and prayer, for it is there that heaven and earth kiss each other! There is much more to come so keep trusting my love and purposes for you! Each day will unfold something of what I have been doing in your life. I will encourage you with a hope that will be daily renewed. Always look up for that is where your salvation is being manifested! Signs and wonders will appear, as they are needed to confirm my truth for you.

Love,
JESUS

1 Peter 1:13-23

[13]*Therefore gird up the loins of your mind, be sober, and rest your hope fully upon the grace that is to be brought to you at the revelation of Jesus Christ;* [14]*as obedient children, not conforming yourselves to the former lusts, as in your ignorance;* [15]*but as He who called you is holy, you also be holy in all your conduct,* [16]*because it is written, "Be holy,*

for I am holy." [17] And if you call on the Father, who without partiality judges according to each one's work, conduct yourselves throughout the time of your stay here in fear; [18] knowing that you were not redeemed with corruptible things, like silver or gold, from your aimless conduct received by tradition from your fathers, [19] but with the precious blood of Christ, as of a lamb without blemish and without spot. [20] He indeed was foreordained before the foundation of the world, but was manifest in these last times for you [21] who through Him believe in God, who raised Him from the dead and gave Him glory, so that your faith and hope are in God. [22] Since you have purified your souls in obeying the truth through the Spirit in sincere love of the brethren, love one another fervently with a pure heart, [23] having been born again, not of corruptible seed but incorruptible, through the word of God which lives and abides forever...

Word Received February 27, 2002

I have opened the doors that cannot be shut and my plans for your life are being carried out. Trust my judgment in all things and listen for my direction! I will set your hearts on fire with a fresh zeal for my Kingdom. Your prayers will be inflamed with a power and enthusiasm never before known. My Holy Spirit will come pouring through them to ignite a revival in the land. Your worship experiences will intensify as I release in you a greater prophetic anointing. I am bringing together a mighty force of believers who are totally entwined in me. Our hearts will beat as one as I set before you what I have planned for this time. Waves of my Spirit will wash over you as you gather in my Name. Get ready for what I have personally crafted for you! It will amaze and delight you. You have cast your bread upon the waters without reservation; now you will see it return to you in magnificent proportions. All that has gone before is only grist for my mill, which is turning out mighty warriors for my Kingdom. There are open heavens above you as I hear and see what is going on in your lives, all of which I have planned for you. I am also becoming more and more part of everything that is taking place. Search out your place in me with an open and willing heart and mind. Do not discount anything that I show you. My vision for you is far greater than anything you could imagine. Every situation and circumstance is serving my purposes in all your lives. Those you bring before me in prayer are those I have chosen to touch with my mercy and purpose. Be obedient to my calling upon your life and I will fulfill it completely! Each person is precious in my eyes and I seek their best. Follow the leading of my Spirit as he guides your steps daily. Be prepared to step into what I am setting before you!

Love,

JESUS

Isaiah 42:8-9

[8] " ... I am the LORD, that is My name; And My glory I will not give to another, Nor My praise to carved images. [9] Behold, the former things have come to pass, And new things I declare; Before they spring forth I tell you of them."

Word Received February 28, 2002

I have broken through the walls that have held you prisoner. I am destroying the works of the evil one. Every structure that has been raised up against my Kingdom is beginning to crumble. The eyes of the blind are being opened to the truth. The lies that have controlled your lives are going out the window. Everything is being worked for my purposes, which will result in true freedom for all who will seek my face. I am stirring things up in order to penetrate hearts with my true love and mercy. Nothing will remain the same as my Spirit comes flooding in to take charge. I am giving a hope and future where there was none. I am destroying the strongholds that have stood in the way of my Kingdom's progress in the lives of my people. Yes, I have chosen you and I will see my choices carried out in your life, come hell or high water. Nothing is going to stand in the way of my will being done in your lives. Everything is about to come to a head. I will no longer tolerate hypocrisy or secrets in the lives of those who are called by my Name. I will expose everything that has been hidden so that my light can shine upon it with healing and restoration. It is a fearful thing to fall into the hands of the living God! Who do you fear more the others or me in your life? I am the only true source of life for you and I will lead you forward into the triumph I have won for you. Now throw yourself upon my mercy and let go everything else that you have been holding on to. It is time to worship the Righteous Father with a true and contrite heart. Enter into the open arms of my love and worship joyfully in my presence! I have been making a way for you into the inner chamber of my heart where healing dwells. I am opening the door for the new things that I have promised. Let my Spirit lead you there!

Love,
JESUS

Isaiah 54:2-5

[2] *"Enlarge the place of your tent, And let them stretch out the curtains of your habitations; Do not spare; Lengthen your cords, And strengthen your stakes.* [3]*For you shall expand to the right and to the left, And your descendants will inherit the nations, And make the desolate cities inhabited.* [4] *"Do not fear, for you will not be ashamed; Neither be disgraced, for you will not be put to shame; For you will forget the shame of your youth, And will not remember the reproach of your widowhood anymore.* [5] *For your Maker is your husband, The LORD of hosts is His name; And your Redeemer is the Holy One of Israel; He is called the God of the whole earth.*

Word Received March 1, 2002

I have opened the windows of heaven and my Spirit will blow through the land! He is calling out to my people to come up higher into the wonder of my glory. My light will cover you like a mantle healing and setting you free. My truth will impact you with a new boldness and wisdom that will carry you forward into the new day ahead. All is forgiven and you are starting fresh in what I have planned for you. Set aside the old ways and enter into the fullness of what I have prepared for you. The Ancient of Days will find unparalleled encounters for you in what lies before you. There is a joining and intertwining of those I have appointed to carry my flame. You will ignite the hearts and minds of those who will receive you for who you are, my beloved friends. There will be a strength and purpose that will come across to others, as you stand firm in the revelation I have given you. My Spirit will communicate volumes in the seeming simple thoughts you will be expressing. You are heralds of my Kingdom declaring my Word to the nations. You will be heard with open ears that I have prepared to receive what I say. Search out my presence wherever you are for I am always there to meet you! Worship the Righteous Father with an enthusiasm and joy that my Spirit gives you! The path ahead will be a straightforward one as the hidden things are exposed and the lies are unearthed. Be aware of your surroundings at all times to see the opportunities I have placed there! My eagles are about to be loosed as the dawn begins to appear on the horizon. The wind of my Spirit is beginning to blow from the east to carry you forward into what I have intended for you. Lay down your lives before me and I will catch you up into the greater things that I have promised. Receive it all in humility and praise!

Love,

JESUS

Psalm 40:1-11,16

[1]I waited patiently for the LORD; And He inclined to me, And heard my cry. [2]He also brought me up out of a horrible pit, Out of the miry clay, And set my feet upon a rock, And established my steps. [3]He has put a new song in my mouth— Praise to our God; Many will see it and fear, And will trust in the LORD. [4]Blessed is that man who makes the LORD his trust, And does not respect the proud, nor such as turn aside to lies. [5]Many, O LORD my God, are Your wonderful works Which You have done; And Your thoughts toward us Cannot be recounted to You in order; If I would declare and speak of them, They are more than can be numbered. [6]Sacrifice and offering You did not desire; My ears You have opened. Burnt offering and sin offering You did not require. [7]Then I said, "Behold, I come; In the scroll of the book it is written of me. [8]I delight to do Your will, O my God, And Your law is within my heart." [9]I have proclaimed the good news

of righteousness In the great congregation.; Indeed, I do not restrain my lips, O LORD, You Yourself know. ¹⁰I have not hidden Your righteousness within my heart; I have declared Your faithfulness and Your salvation; I have not concealed Your lovingkindness and Your truth From the great congregation. ¹¹Do not withhold Your tender mercies from me, O LORD; Let Your lovingkindness and Your truth continually preserve me. ¹⁶Let all those who seek You rejoice and be glad in You; Let such as love Your salvation say continually, "The LORD be magnified!"

Word Received March 2, 2002

I have released my Spirit among you in a fresh and exciting way that will intoxicate you with joy and gladness. Healing and restoration of lives and relationships will be on the increase. I have destroyed the yokes of bondage once and for all. The anointing of my Spirit has sealed you in an everlasting covenant that will not be broken. You will move higher and higher into the places I have established for you to go. They will encompass many and varied expressions of my purposes for you. Great and open opportunities await you as my Spirit leads you into them. My favor and provision are sufficient for all your needs. I will follow-through in everything I give you to do. It will be my working in and through you that will accomplish everything to my honor and praise. Look for the moments we can be apart together where I can replenish you for the next steps you will be taking. Enter into your worship of the Ancient of Days as a time of intimacy with our majesty. Let the beauty of our holiness surround you and imbue you with new strength. We will enfold you in our arms and hold you close. All our love is being poured out upon you. Take hold of it for I am speaking into you a fresh revelation of the truth that will set free all who will follow after me! I am angry over the lies that have held you captive to the wiles of the evil one. This is why the way has been shown to you to come out of his control. Take full advantage of every opportunity that I give you to bring release. I am building up my Kingdom with those who have been liberated from their past. I am bringing their future into play very quickly. Even the shadows will dissipate as my light shines down from above. I have removed the grave clothes so you can freely move in the wonder of my Kingdom. It is the year of jubilee!

Love,

JESUS

Proverbs 3:5-6

⁵Trust in the LORD with all your heart, And lean not on your own understanding; ⁶In all your ways acknowledge Him, And He shall direct your paths.

Word Received March 3, 2002

The flaming sword of my Spirit is about to be revealed to you in the fullness of its power. It will appear in your midst with a flourish cutting through the flesh to the dividing of bone and marrow. It will release you from bondage and set you free to enjoy all that I have for you. The trumpets will sound carrying a note of liberation for all who believe in me. Hearts will be opened to the fresh wind of my Spirit, which is blowing through the atmosphere. A holy trembling will come upon you as I catch you up into the wonder of my Kingdom. You are stepping into a whole new way of being as my loyal subjects. It will not be a matter of pride on your part but a confidence that I have placed in the inward parts. You will speak as a royal spokesman for my Kingdom. You carry my authority, which is in perfect submission to the Ancient of Days. It will flow through your worship of the Righteous Father as you gather in the triumph of my Resurrection. I am moving you forward in the places I have assigned to you. It is there that you will find prosperity for your souls and for your bodies. I have appropriated the riches of the earth for the extension of my Kingdom among you. There will be a new boldness as you take charge of what I have given you to do. There will be a core of the committed that have caught my vision for this time. They will mount up with wings like eagles as they soar in the presence of my glory. You belong to me as a royal priesthood who will do mighty exploits in my Name and to my honor. Your reach will extend far beyond your grasp for I am declaring my purposes to the nations. I am setting everything in my order and you will be made to fit the position I have established for you. Trust my will for your life and let my Holy Spirit take you where I want you to go! Ho!

Love,

JESUS

Hebrews 12:28-29

28Therefore, since we are receiving a kingdom which cannot be shaken, let us have grace, by which we may serve God acceptably with reverence and godly fear. 29For our God is a consuming fire.

Word Received March 4, 2002

I walk before you guiding your steps and opening doors. I am with you to make you wise in all that is taking place. I am establishing you in my purposes and plans. Wait with anticipation for what I will be revealing to you! All things are in my hands and I am putting many things together for you. I have anointed you to carry out what I have called you to do. You are in place as a part of the move of my Spirit into the world scene. I am empowering you to carry out what I have intended for this time. Today you will catch glimpses of what I am talking about as you carry out your appointed tasks. Everything is significant to me and everything has my attention. Continue to draw closer to me even in the public places of your life. My worship goes on inside of you as well as outside of you. We are continually connected and our relationship is far deeper than you can imagine. My Spirit flows through like a river nourishing everything around you. He is impacting everyone you touch with a word, a gesture or even a smile. Know that you are an integral part of my Kingdom and everything you are involved in includes my input. I will prosper your effort on my behalf, for that is what will draw the outsiders to come inside. All that you do is holy to me for it all expresses my partnership with you.

Listen for my voice as I express myself in your thoughts and trust what I am saying to you there. Put it into action as my Spirit in you grasps a hold of it! Every day is precious in my sight and I give it all to you to enjoy and to participate with me in it. The way is open for you to achieve what I have prepared for you. See it with the eyes of faith and not depend on your own understanding alone. Many things are in process as my final plans are being solidified. Reality and truth are the same to me. Ho!

Love,
JESUS

Lamentations 3:22-24

22Through the LORD's mercies we are not consumed, Because His compassions fail not. 23They are new every morning; Great is Your faithfulness. 24"The LORD is my portion," says my soul, "Therefore I hope in Him!"

Word Received March 5, 2002

My Kingdom comes with power and life for all those who receive it with faith and joy. I have presented you with it as a gift of my mercy and love. Relinquish your fears and enter into the fullness of my grace as you follow the leading of my Spirit. He will transform your life into the masterpiece that I intended it to be. Continue walking in the way I have provided for you. Take each day as my opportunity to manifest my glory in and through you. Take hold of it with a ferocious desire to see my goodness in the land of the living. Storm the walls of hypocrisy and unbelief, and tear them down with my Resurrection power that resides in you. You are to move ahead in the things that truly matter under the command of my Holy Spirit. I have provided the partners for your journey and they carry the anointing I have given them. Some have been with you through the past struggles, and others are coming alongside to join you in the triumphant march that is before you. The ways and means of my Kingdom are totally at your disposal. Use them in good faith with the confirming presence of my

Spirit. You are being covered with a new mantle of worship that will extend you further into the inner sanctuary where the Ancient of Days abides in the fullness of his majesty. You are growing in the grace that I have poured out upon you. Every need will be met according to the richness of my treasure that has been opened to you. Step out with a fresh boldness in what I am opening before you! Do not hesitate to soar into the future that I am giving you. As eagles you are no longer earth bound, for you are free to rise above the mountaintops to see beyond the present. I am awakening my people to the destiny that I have instilled in them. Come up higher and see the wonders I have in store for you!

Love,
JESUS

Ecclesiastes 3:9-14

⁹What profit has the worker from that in which he labors? ¹⁰I have seen the God-given task with which the sons of men are to be occupied. ¹¹He has made everything beautiful in its time. Also He has put eternity in their hearts, except that no one can find out the work that God does from beginning to end. *¹²I know that nothing is better for them than to rejoice, and to do good in their lives, ¹³and also that every man should eat and drink and enjoy the good of all his labor—it is the gift of God. ¹⁴I know that whatever God does, It shall be forever. Nothing can be added to it, And nothing taken from it. God does it, that men should fear before Him.*

Word Received March 6, 2002

I am raising my banner over you as a sign of my promise in you. I have called you into the ranks of my followers to fulfill my purposes on the earth. I have anointed you with the oil of gladness that is far superior to anything the world can give you. It is filled with my Resurrection power to carry out mighty exploits in my Name. It is my acting in and through you by the presence of my Holy Spirit who holds the reins in your life. He is the manifest glory of my truth and authority for you. His ways are my ways, which produces great fruit in you for my Kingdom. Do not measure the value of things by what you see for my views are different than yours. Even the smallest detail can carry great weight for me and the larger things may not be as important. What I desire is faithfulness in the inner parts where I hold court in the intimacy we have between us. Your worship has great acclaim in heaven as it rises up to the Ancient of Days. When you seek my face with your whole heart everything else fades into the background. Trust my evaluation of what is going on rather than your own! Follow the leading of my Spirit in you as you hear my thoughts coming to mind. I will show you great and marvelous things as you continue along the path I have set for you. Do not discount anything that is happening for it all has a purpose in my eternal plan. Draw closer in your quiet moments and do not be distracted by what is unimportant to me. I have planted my seed of salvation in you and it is growing even when you sleep. It is not by effort that it grows but by my presence in you guiding your journey. The fire of my Spirit is penetrating the darkness setting the captives free from their bondage. The lies that have encircled you are being broken one by one until all of my will is accomplished.

Love,
JESUS

Psalm 46

¹God is our refuge and strength, A very present help in trouble. ²Therefore we will not fear, Though the earth be removed, And though the mountains be carried into the midst of the sea; ³Though its waters roar and be troubled, Though the mountains shake with its swelling. Selah ⁴There is a river whose streams shall make glad the city of God, The holy place of the tabernacle of the Most High. ⁵God is in the midst of her, she shall not be moved; God shall help her, just at the break of dawn. ⁶The nations raged, the kingdoms were moved; He uttered His voice, the earth melted. ⁷The LORD of hosts is with us; The God of Jacob is our refuge. Selah ⁸Come, behold the works of the LORD, Who has made desolations in the earth. ⁹He makes wars cease to the end of the earth; He breaks the bow and cuts the spear in two; He burns the chariot in the fire. ¹⁰Be still, and know that I am God; I will be exalted among the nations, I will be exalted in the earth! ¹¹The LORD of hosts is with us; The God of Jacob is our refuge. Selah

Word Received March 7, 2002

My joy will explode in you as my Spirit gathers you up into the holy of holies where my presence is revealed. It is the place of intimacy and worship where our hearts are joined in the true kiss of peace. It is the journey that I have given you, which will bear great fruit in your life. Many will come to know me as you follow my leading in all that you do. You will be opening wells of living water wherever you go. Lean into the wind of my Spirit and let it carry you forward into the challenges and opportunities I have for you. Each small step you take in my Name will be a giant step for my Kingdom. Trust what I am pouring into you and allow the new wine to ferment in your wineskin. The results will be intoxicating with the freshness of the new day that is dawning upon you. I will satisfy your needs as you continue in the direction I have set for your life. Some things will remain hidden until the time is appropriate for you to see them. In the meanwhile keep moving on the path that is before you. I will prosper your efforts as well as bring forth surprises from time to time. I will open the way before you into an open field where the fullness of my freedom is experienced. It will flow from your willingness to be in submission to my Holy Spirit in all areas in your life. He will take you to mountaintops and through the valleys. He will go ahead of you and he will stand behind you for he is your strength and wisdom. There is much that lies ahead of you and you have already entered into the time of change, which I have been promising. By the time it is finished nothing will remain unchanged and all of it for your best interests. My people who are called by my Name will rise to the occasion, as my will is unfolded before them. There will be a drawing together of hearts and lives like never before seen on the earth!

Love,
JESUS

Psalm 47

¹Oh, clap your hands, all you peoples! Shout to God with the voice of triumph! ²For the LORD Most High is awesome; He is a great King over all the earth. ³He will subdue the peoples under us, And the nations under our feet. ⁴He will choose our inheritance for us, The excellence of Jacob whom He loves. Selah ⁵God has gone up with a shout, The

LORD with the sound of a trumpet. ⁶Sing praises to God, sing praises! Sing praises to our King, sing praises! ⁷For God is the King of all the earth; Sing praises with understanding. ⁸God reigns over the nations; God sits on His holy throne. ⁹The princes of the people have gathered together, The people of the God of Abraham. For the shields of the earth belong to God; He is greatly exalted.

Word Received March 8, 2002

The wonder of my glory will burst upon you in the tantalizing array of our majesty. We will meet with you in a holy convocation of our making. We will transform the moments and the days with the fullness of our love and joy. We will wash you in the healing waters of our mercy and compassion. All that we have intended for you will come into being as you follow the leading of our Holy Spirit in you. He has charge of your life with all the elements we have put into it. Your expectations will be surpassed by the reality of our plans for you. All things will fall into place as you enter the covenant relationship of worship with the Ancient of Days. It is there that we become one as heaven and earth kiss in the deepest intimacy. Signs of our favor will shower down upon you as you proceed in the events of my Kingdom. The growing edge of our purposes in your life is bearing fruit in what we have determined for this time. Keep your focus on what we are revealing to you in thought, words and actions! We are slowly unveiling the future we have promised you. The substance and value of it will astound you. Receive it with an open and grateful heart! There will be radical changes occurring all around you as you faithfully follow after me. I have set many things in motion as we draw closer to the final outpouring of my Spirit. He will come like the latter rain to make the fields ready for the great harvest of souls for my Kingdom. You will see more and more evidence of what I have been preparing for this time. There will be things happening for you personally that will produce great joy in your own life. I am raising up my standard on the earth so my people can be gathered to it as a point of confidence and release. You are entering the final phases of the great awakening on the earth. Get ready for it!

Love,

JESUS

Revelation 19:6-10

⁶And I heard, as it were, the voice of a great multitude, as the sound of many waters and as the sound of mighty thunderings, saying, "Alleluia! For the Lord God Omnipotent reigns! ⁷Let us be glad and rejoice and give Him glory, for the marriage of the Lamb has come, and His wife has made herself ready." ⁸And to her it was granted to be arrayed in fine linen, clean and bright, for the fine linen is the righteous acts of the saints. ⁹Then he said to me, "Write: 'Blessed are those who are called to the marriage supper of the Lamb!'" And he said to me, "These are the true sayings of God." ¹⁰And I fell at his feet to worship him. But he said to me, "See that you do not do that! I am your fellow servant, and of your brethren who have the testimony of Jesus. Worship God! For the testimony of Jesus is the spirit of prophecy."

Word Received March 9, 2002

I have opened the door to the future that I have planned for you. My Holy Spirit is leading you through it as he guides your steps. Trust his wisdom and listen for his direction! I am unfolding many opportunities for you to serve my Kingdom. Sometimes it may seem that you are involved in only ordinary things, but they, too, serve my purposes. Everything has its place in my plans. I am about to introduce you to a new level of worship as I draw you closer to the Ancient of Days. He will lift you up into the rarest of atmospheres where you will encounter the beauty of his majesty. It is the experience of the true Father's love for you. He will bestow his blessing upon you. It will anoint you for mighty exploits in my Name. I will move heaven and earth to carry out his will for my people. Continue to seek my face with an attitude of humility and grace for I am with you! I have sown the seeds of my mercy throughout your life and now you will see the results. You will not become overly concerned about tomorrow just enjoy what I give you today. Proceed with what I place before you and leave the rest to me! I am the healer and restorer. Trust that I will accomplish all of it!

Love,
JESUS

Psalm 119:2
²Blessed are those who keep His testimonies, Who seek Him with the whole heart!

Word Received March 10, 2002

The fire of my Spirit will be unleashed among you to transform you for my glory. I will put my truth in the center of your being to set you free to worship the Heavenly Father in sincerity and joy. My love is being poured out like a waterfall covering you with my favor. Seek my face with a fresh enthusiasm and zeal as my Spirit carries you along in my river of life! The burdens and the chains will fall from you and I will bring you into a new day where my peace reigns supreme. Receive and believe what I have prepared for you! I am healing the wounds of your heart and lifting the grief from your souls. Turn to me with your whole being and let go of what was! Trust my will for your life as I lead you into the fulfillment of it all! I have sown the seeds of life in you and now is the time for the harvest to take place. I am gathering you, into my presence and surrounding you with my chosen and anointed. Together you will produce much fruit for my Kingdom. It is time for you to take your rightful place in me. Your wanderings are over and I am bringing you home. The eyes of the blind are being opened and the lame will walk in the ways of my righteousness. All my promises are coming into play in your life as I draw you closer to the Ancient of Days. The trumpets will sound as you give him a royal welcome into your midst. He will lift you up beyond the present moment into a place of his own designation. Yield to him as my Spirit carries you forward into the tomorrow I have planned for you. Singleness of heart and devotion are the keys that will open the future I have for you. You will succeed and prosper in everything I give you! Today is the time of your salvation, which has been prophesied from the beginning. The wind of my Spirit has begun to blow with greater intensity!

Love,
JESUS

Psalm 51:10-12

[10]Create in me a clean heart, O God, And renew a steadfast spirit within me. [11]Do not cast me away from Your presence, And do not take Your Holy Spirit from me. [12]Restore to me the joy of Your salvation, And uphold me by Your generous Spirit.

Word Received March 11, 2002

I have awakened the sleeping giant, and my Holy Spirit will be leading you forward. His fire will inspire you and give you the abilities to carry out the mission I have set for you. Trust his direction in you and be open to what he shows you to do! He is the source and resource of all that you will be asked to do. His will is binding on your life. Let him carry you along the road that I have set for you! His wind will be at your back and his pillar of fire will go before you. There will be a harmony in everything that will be taking place. There will be many open doors for you to go through as you follow my leading for the rest of your life. I will be reducing the stress and the strife for they serve no purpose for the increase of my Kingdom among you. I am placing you on the high ground of victory where you can see the defeat of the enemy forces below. You are a worshipper of the Most High God and you carry his banners wherever you go. Enter again and again into the inner court of my presence, and experience the refreshing and renewal that I have for you there. Always approach my throne of grace with confidence and trust! My mercy seat is always accessible to you and it is my delight to have you meet me there. I will follow through in everything I have given you. You will see the hidden things begin to surface so that my hand can rest upon them. I will give you wisdom and understanding in all of it. I have placed you where you are for my purposes and for my plans. My Kingdom is unfolding in the power and expression of my truth. My cause is advancing on every front and you are in the forefront of what I am doing. You will be experiencing my joy and peace at the center of everything that is happening. What lies ahead of you will be all for my glory. Rest in me and let my Spirit guide you all the way!

Love,
JESUS

Psalm 52:8-9

8But I am like a green olive tree in the house of God; I trust in the mercy of God forever and ever. 9I will praise You forever, Because You have done it; And in the presence of Your saints I will wait on Your name, for it is good.

Word Received March 12, 2002

The tongues of fire will lick up the blood on the altar of your sacrifice of praise. The glory of my presence will surround you there. You will experience the fullness of my favor and you will find the true freedom of my Kingdom. It is all a gift that I joyfully bestow upon you who are called by my Name. I am finalizing the plans that I have set for this time, and you will begin to see my purposes more clearly played out in your life. Embrace my will in all that you are doing and follow through what I give you! Your focus of worship as the center of your life is pleasing to the Heavenly Father, and he joins with you in it. Heaven and earth are not so far apart and the veil between is often penetrated. My sacrifice of the cross has torn it apart so you can easily come before the Ancient of Days with your prayers and petitions. He hears them and answers you since they proceed from the heart he has put in you. Indeed, they are the expressions of his intentions for all that he seeks to do on the earth. Your partnership with him is vital to what will be happening in the coming days. The reign of my Kingdom is established in you, and is expanding throughout the earth through all who have surrendered their hearts to me. I am sowing the seeds of truth everywhere and they are taking root in places you least expect. My Holy Spirit will be poured out like the latter rain and the harvest will quickly follow. The doors are opening for you and my Spirit is walking you through them. He knows the outcome from the beginning so he knows exactly how to guide you. Let him lead you step by step even when you don't feel or completely understand what is happening. Trust his judgment above your own in every circumstance! What may seem to be unimportant to you may be radically significant for him.

Love,
JESUS

Hebrews 13:20-21
20Now may the God of peace who brought up our Lord Jesus from the dead, that great Shepherd of the sheep, through the blood of the everlasting covenant, 21make you complete in every good work to do His will, working in you what is well pleasing in His sight, through Jesus Christ, to whom be glory forever and ever. Amen.

Word Received March 13, 2002

I have opened the door that will not be shut as my will is being done in every person and every situation. Rely upon my judgment and on my revelation for it is sound and timely! I will guide you in everything that I present to you. I will show you the way to go and what to say when the opportunities arise. I am using everything to further my Kingdom as the time of my coming draws closer. I am opening the eyes of the blind and tearing the veils off those who have been deceived. Follow my leading as I direct you in what I have planned for you. Rest in the assurance that you are on the right path even when things become somewhat difficult! The outcome will be successful on every occasion. Proceed with what I give you and take charge of what I have chosen for you! The light of my truth is dawning, making many things clear for you. My Spirit is bringing a newfound confidence and boldness to your life. He is unfolding before you a whole new way of looking at things, which will produce much fruit in the days ahead. Continue to be open to the attitude of worship that is growing within you! Lift up my Name in praise and wonder as I appear in your gatherings! My Spirit has broken through into the very heart of your being to release what I have placed there for you. It is a time of small triumphs, which will grow into a mighty victory for you and for my Kingdom. Approach everything with an open and expectant heart seeking my purposes in it! I will show you what I have been holding for you. The changes that are coming will redirect what you thought was your destiny. Your future is in my hands and it carries with it a hope for greater things than you can imagine. Listen for my voice even in the center of the confusion that may be around you. Get ready for what I have for you!

Love,
JESUS

Micah 6:8
⁸He has shown you, O man, what is good; And what does the LORD require of you But to do justly, To love mercy, And to walk humbly with your God?

Word Received March 14, 2002

I am lighting the fires of revival on the mountaintops for all to see. They will be beacons drawing the lost to me as my Spirit is there with the fullness of his power. Healing favor will be available to all who come to me with an open and willing heart. I will carry out the plans of the Righteous Father in all beauty and holiness. Trust my compassion towards you and for all who stand in need before me! I am summoning the people from every direction to come and follow me to the place of consecration and life for them. I will withhold no good thing from your lives as I pour out my blessings upon you. I am removing the distractions that have sought to deter you from your primary goals. Seek my face with deeper and ever increasing passion for my Kingdom! Worship the Ancient of Days with greater abandonment as my Spirit catches you up into the wonder of my presence. It is there you will find the intimacy with me that you have been longing for since the beginning of our relationship. There is a mantle of authority upon you that will be recognized as you speak under the anointing of my Holy Spirit. He will supply everything you will need to do my will in your life, and for those that you serve in my Name. I am placing you in positions of greater opportunity for the glory of my Kingdom. All that you will be doing will reflect my honor and grace in your life. Your partnership with those I have called is established and will be growing as you move along the path I have given you. Always seek out my purposes at the center of what is happening! Listen for a clear sound of my voice in whatever is taking place! I am directing your steps and guiding your allegiances. I am building a confidence in you that will enable you to take charge of situations as they arise. Always trust me in it!

Love,
JESUS

Matthew 11:28-30

28"Come to Me, all you who labor and are heavy laden, and I will give you rest. 29Take My yoke upon you and learn from Me, for I am gentle and lowly in heart, and you will find rest for your souls. 30For My yoke is easy and My burden is light."

Word Received March 15, 2002

The fire of my righteousness will burst forth upon the earth and my truth will be fully revealed. The shadows will be dispersed and everyone will see clearly what is taking place. The hidden things will be disclosed, some for commendation and the others for conviction. I will always ultimately have my way. The Heavenly Father watches over you with his grace and mercy. He will restore what was lost and bring many things together that have been separated. My love will flow over it all, covering it with my peace and hope. Your place has been set at the table that I have prepared for this time. It is a banquet in my presence where you can rejoice and celebrate my goodness toward you. It is a place of true worship of the Ancient of Day in the fullness of his majesty. Bow down before him and enjoy all that he is giving you! It is a time of healing for the hearts that have been wounded and the lives that have been broken. Focus on what I have placed before you and leave the rest for me to take care of according to my will! I have opened the door for you to walk through to where I have intended you to go. It will occupy all of your attention so you will not be distracted by what is happening with those who are not your concern. My reach and purposes are far greater than you could ever imagine. The whole earth is under my command and direction. I will guide the nations and the events that are taking place. Continue to pray and to speak as my Holy Spirit leads you! All of your life has been in my hands, and I will not leave you now in the crucial moments that lie before you. The plan of the Righteous Father is being worked out to his perfection. There is a radical movement of my Spirit coming, which will bring about revolutionary changes. Be attentive to what you will be doing with him in it!

Love,
JESUS

Isaiah 61:10-11

[10]I will greatly rejoice in the LORD, My soul shall be joyful in my God; For He has clothed me with the garments of salvation, He has covered me with the robe of righteousness, As a bridegroom decks himself with ornaments, And as a bride adorns herself with her jewels. [11]For as the earth brings forth its bud, As the garden causes the things that are sown in it to spring forth, So the Lord GOD will cause righteousness and praise to spring forth before all the nations.

Word Received March 16, 2002

The trumpets will sound and my glory will come down to surround you with my love. I have set you apart to enter into the fullness of my purposes. There is more to come as you follow after me. I will lead you through the strongholds of the enemy into the open fields of my freedom. I am partnering you with many who have heard my call and have entered into a covenant of righteousness with me. There are many pretenders, but the light that comes down from above will expose them. Your place is to listen for my voice and follow through with what I am revealing to you. I will always minister heart to heart with the plans of my Kingdom. I will show you everything you will need to know to carry out my will for you. The anointing power of my Holy Spirit will enable you to see, speak and do what the Righteous Father has commanded for you. There are things coming that may not always be clear to you but trust me anyway. I will bring everything into focus for you as you move ahead in what I am giving you. Take each day as an opportunity to see my goodness in the land of the living! The wind of my Spirit will begin to blow gently before it becomes a gale force. I will catch you up in it to soar into my presence, where heaven and earth are transformed into an eternal moment with the Ancient of Days. Your worship there will be filled with the roar of my waterfall of grace pouring down upon you. Your soul and body will be flooded with my life-giving light. Healing will occur instantly and the debris of the past washed away in a moment. You will come forth new-born and renewed by my Spirit in you. It will all take place in the twinkling of an eye when you least expect it. Like a river it will carry you into the eternal joy of my Kingdom. Reach out to me with open arms and an open heart!

Love,
JESUS

Philippians 1:9-11

[9]And this I pray, that your love may abound still more and more in knowledge and all discernment, [10]that you may approve the things that are excellent, that you may be sincere and without offense till the day of Christ, [11]being filled with the fruits of righteousness which are by Jesus Christ, to the glory and praise of God.

Word Received March 18, 2002

The flames of fire will consume the remains of the evil one. His forces are being turned upon themselves in their defeat. I have established my victory among you and you will be enjoying the spoils. My favor is with you as you pass through the debris that is floating around you. The destruction of the strongholds is complete as you move into the positions I have established for you. My presence surrounds you with joy and gladness as you move ahead in the plans of the Righteous Father. The way is cleared for you to take your rightful place in my Kingdom. You are seeing the manifestation of my healing power, as I reach out and touch those that you encounter on your journey with me. The waves created by my Spirit will rapidly spread throughout the earth. He is changing the face of history as he impacts the events that are taking place. He is raising up those I have called to succeed in their holy appointments. The resistance is wavering and beginning to fall before them. Trust my wisdom for you and follow where my Spirit is leading you, for he knows your destination! The doors are still open and you will be going through them with a flourish and a shout. Get ready, for you have only touched the hem of my garment of praise! You are about to be gathered into a worship experience that will truly blow your minds. You will see the crystal sea for yourself, as you appear before the heavenly throne room in the anointing of my Spirit. It will be a radical turn of events for you personally, and corporately for all who are joined with you in it. There is a fresh flow of my Spirit, which will carry you far beyond anything you have known up until this point. Be prepared for the inevitable triumph of my Holy Spirit in your life! There is much more waiting for you just beyond the horizon of your vision.

Love,
JESUS

Isaiah 62:1-3
¹For Zion's sake I will not hold My peace, And for Jerusalem's sake I will not rest, Until her righteousness goes forth as brightness, And her salvation as a lamp that burns. ²The Gentiles shall see your righteousness, And all kings your glory. You shall be called by a new name, Which the mouth of the LORD will name. ³You shall also be

a crown of glory In the hand of the LORD, And a royal diadem In the hand of your God.

Word Received March 19, 2002

Fly away with me into the heavenly places where we can meet face to face. Join with those who worship the Righteous Father with a true heart and an honest desire. Rest in the assurance of my love as I direct your paths to the outcome that I have planned for your life! I will show you clearly what I will for your life as you follow the leading of my Spirit in you. It is not always a matter of understanding, but of relying upon me for all your needs. I have your best interests at heart and I will always show you the better way. Seek my face in prayer and devotion, surrendering to my wisdom for you! I will supply the strength to carry out the plans I have made for you. The fire of my Spirit will stir up in you a new level of commitment to my purposes for you. My Kingdom comes with power and light to endorse what I am doing in your life. Proceed on what is at hand and take one step at a time! The wave of my Spirit is building to a crescendo in your walk with me. There will be more radical changes coming, with tremendous outpourings of signs and wonders for my people. You are slowly coming into your own as you lean into the wind of my Spirit. He will take you to new heights in our relationship together. He will bring many alongside of you who have caught the fresh vision I have for this time. I will saturate your days with my presence even in the most mundane of situations. Heaven and earth will become entwined in the passion of my favor. Do not be discouraged for I will take everything and turn it for my favorable results! Even now I am pulling many things together which you were not even aware were happening. There is much to come, which will produce a great harvest for my Kingdom. Continually pray that my will be done in your life and in the lives of those that I present before you!

Love,
JESUS

Philippians 2:12-13
²Therefore, my beloved, as you have always obeyed, not as in my presence only, but now much more in my absence, work out your own salvation with fear and trembling; ¹³for it is God who works in you both to will and to do for His good pleasure.

Word Received March 20, 2002

I have opened the gates of my Kingdom that all may enter into my presence. My desire is for the hearts of all to be turned to me to receive the fullness of my love. I am destroying the works of the evil one as you declare my truth with confidence and boldness. I am removing the hindrances to your walk with me. Your times of worship with me will become even more glorious than it has ever been. You are mounting up with wings like eagles and soaring to new heights with the Righteous Father and me. The Ancient of Days has become a constant companion through the intercession of my Spirit. I am drawing you closer to those I have called for this time in your life. Some have always been there and others are coming alongside as you continue the journey I have set before you. Trust my wisdom and my selection for I know what lies ahead of you! My trumpets are sounding the call that will bring you from seeming defeat to total victory. See with the eyes of faith what I have prepared for you and joyfully embrace it all! There is an ebb and a flow to my Spirit, but know that it will always move you further ahead than where you were. I am beginning to wake up many who have fallen asleep or who have been distracted by their own concerns. I will provide for every need that you have according to my riches and plan. Things are happening even though you are not aware of them. My work goes on at many levels and in many locations. The will of the Heavenly Father is at the center of it all. The light of my new day is dawning and many will come to it with willing and open hearts. The multitudes are beginning to shift their allegiance to my Kingdom. My love will be transforming everyone and everything that you touch in my Name. Your prayers herald my authority that is over the whole earth!

Love,
JESUS

1 Thessalonians 5:16
[16]Rejoice always,

Word Received March 21, 2002

The trumpets will sound and my eagles will gather to take flight into the heavenly realms of my presence. My Spirit is being released in a fresh and mighty way among my people. Healing and restoration will be the children's bread as they eat to my glory. My purposes will transform the direction you have been going, making it conform more closely to my will for you. Open doors and open windows await you as the opportunities and the blessings will present themselves. Keep your focus on me and enter joyfully into the glorious moments of worship and celebration. It is there that we are joined together and I can impart a greater awareness of who I am. The dawn of my new day is breaking on the horizon as the light of my truth becomes more apparent to all who receive it. I am enlightening you with new insights into my revelation knowledge. The veils of the past are being quickly removed so you can see with a fresh clarity of vision. There is much yet to come and it will come in ways that will amaze you. All the changes that will be taking place will bring you to a whole new stage of life. Your yielding to the leading of my Holy Spirit will bring you into a totally new chapter for your life. He knows what the Righteous Father has planned for you, and now he will bring you there. Trust his wisdom and guidance, for it will bring you into a place of great freedom and peace! He is renewing you in body, soul and spirit for what lies ahead. Your partnership in my Kingdom will bring much honor to my Name. You will find the satisfaction you always longed for and there will be many who will share in the wonder of it. Be still and wait upon me! Do not become anxious or try to rush ahead of what I have prepared for you! It will all happen in my good time!

Love,
JESUS

Proverbs 16:9
⁹*A man's heart plans his way, But the LORD directs his steps.*

Word Received March 24, 2002

The fire of my righteousness will expand the universe of my truth among you. I will inflame your worship into a new dimension of joy and gladness. I will triumph mightily in your midst as I bring you forward into a great and open place of my freedom. All that has gone before is washed in the purity of my appointed Word to you. I am speaking to your heart and opening the expectant hope I have for you. I have crushed the enemy under your feet and I have taken from him what little power had been left to him. Your place in my Kingdom has raised you far above all the principalities and powers that have tried to enslave you. Acknowledge my Name and trust in my love and you too will triumph mightily! You have become a force to be reckoned with as the fullness of my Holy Spirit takes the lead in your life. Apart from me you can do nothing, but with me all things are possible. I have destroyed the yokes of bondage with the anointing of my Holy Spirit. Keep the eyes of your heart focused on me for I alone am your salvation! I am putting many things together as the time of my visitation draws closer. The wind of my Spirit is increasing in power as that great and marvelous day approaches. Let it carry you to new heights of intimacy and peace with me. The eagles are rising up and circling over the gathering places I have established for them. Get ready to enter into what I have prepared for you! The doors are open and by my Spirit you are crossing over the threshold. It is the truly new day that I have promised for you. The old is past and the best of the rest of your life has now begun. Follow me into it! It is in the inundation of my Holy Spirit who is flooding your mind, soul and body with the fulfillment of my Kingdom authority. Receive it all with a truly believing and grateful heart!

Love,
JESUS

Psalm 63

¹*O God, You are my God; Early will I seek You; My soul thirsts for You; My flesh longs for You In a dry and thirsty land Where there is no water. ²So I have looked for You in the sanctuary, To see Your power and Your glory. ³Because Your lovingkindness is better than life, My lips shall praise You. ⁴Thus I will bless You while I live; I will lift up my hands in Your name. ⁵My soul shall be satisfied as with marrow and fatness, And my mouth shall praise You with joyful lips. ⁶When I remember You on my bed, I meditate on You in the night watches. ⁷Because You have been my help, Therefore in the shadow of Your wings I will rejoice. ⁸My soul follows close behind You; Your right hand upholds me. ⁹But those who seek my life, to destroy it, Shall go into the lower parts of the earth. ¹⁰They shall fall by the sword; They shall be a portion for jackals. ¹¹But the king shall rejoice in God; Everyone who swears by Him shall glory; But the mouth of those who speak lies shall be stopped.*

Word Received March 25, 2002

I have walked you through into a whole new place of being with me. I will show you great and marvelous things in the days ahead. I have chosen you for much more than you realize, and it will all come together at the appropriate time. I am partnering you with many who have answered my call in the deep and quiet moments I have had with them. It is not so much a matter of seeking, but of waiting on me for what I have in store for you. As always nothing is wasted, everything has a proper order in the things of the Kingdom. My ways will often circumvent the ordinary ways of doing things. I like to operate in the unexpected and the unusual. Still there is a flow to what I make happen. There is an underlying harmony that can only be perceived in the depths of my grace. I am reaffirming and reestablishing the power base that I have given you. It is my Holy Spirit who carries out my will in your life. He speaks with the authority of the Ancient of Days for they are in unity, even as I am one with them. There will always be a witness to it in your heart as my Spirit dwells there, too. Keep your focus on worship alive at all times, for it is there that you are renewed by the testimony of my Spirit with you! I am building up my people in a very special way to exhibit to the world what my true intentions are for them. I desire all people to come into the knowledge of my truth so as to find their true place with me. I am disclosing the lies they have believed so they can be set free by my revelation in their hearts. It is what I am working through you as well. I am restoring everything that was lost when the enemy attacked you. You are fast becoming the new creation that I planned you to be. I am uniting you with those I have chosen for this end time experience. You will always be one among equals!

Love,
JESUS

1 Peter 2:9-10

⁹But you are a chosen generation, a royal priesthood, a holy nation, His own special people, that you may proclaim the praises of Him who called you out of darkness into His marvelous light; ¹⁰who once were not a people but are now the people of God, who had not obtained mercy but now have obtained mercy.

Word Received March 26, 2002

Rest in me and allow my Spirit to carry you where I will today! What happens is up to me and I have your best interests at heart. I also know the end from the beginning so trust my judgment for you! Do not lose focus, but concentrate even more diligently on what I reveal to you! What I have in store for those who love me will be far greater than anyone could ever imagine. I will be turning many things around for those who have not responded to my call. I will awaken them out of their confusion and unbelief. You meanwhile must continue in the direction I have assigned to you. I will supply what is needed and open the doors that I have intended for you. Take the moments to look up and see the windows of opportunity I have provided for you! Engage in worship in spite of what you may feel like at the moment. Step off the cliff of indecision and allow the wind of my Spirit to lift you up into the heights of my joy and clarity. Show yourself approved in what I give you to carry out in my Name. It is all my doing from beginning to end. You are standing in my favor even when there are momentary lapses in what you think should be happening. Always come back to me and let my presence wash over you to cleanse you from the accumulation of frustration that sometimes appears. Cast caution to the winds and launch out again into the freedom I have established for you! Seek me in the center of what you are experiencing for I am with you there! I am unveiling the authority I have placed upon you as well as my anointing to apply it where I see fit. Your days are in my hands and I will do with them what the Righteous Father commands. Sometimes there is a momentary parting of the ways while I take care of what was left undone. Then you will return to the purposes I have set for you!

Love,

JESUS

Psalm 65

¹Praise is awaiting You, O God, in Zion; And to You the vow shall be performed. ²O You who hear prayer, To You all flesh will come. ³Iniquities prevail against me; As for our transgressions, You will provide atonement for them. ⁴Blessed is the man You choose, And cause to approach You, That he may dwell in Your courts. We shall be satisfied with the goodness of Your house, Of Your holy temple. ⁵By awesome deeds in righteousness You will answer us, O God of our salvation, You who are the confidence of all the ends of the earth, And of the far-off seas; ⁶Who established the mountains by His strength, Being clothed with power; ⁷You who still the noise of the seas, The noise of their waves, And the tumult of the peoples. ⁸They also who dwell in the farthest parts are afraid of Your signs; You make the outgoings of the morning and evening rejoice. ⁹You visit the earth and water it, You greatly enrich it; The river of God is full of water; You provide their grain, For so You have prepared it. ¹⁰You water its ridges abundantly, You settle its furrows; You make it soft with showers, You bless its growth. ¹¹You crown the year with Your goodness, And Your paths drip with abundance. ¹²They drop on the pastures of the wilderness, And the little hills rejoice on every side. ¹³The pastures are clothed with flocks; The valleys also are covered with grain; They shout for joy, they also sing.

Word Received March 27, 2002

The wind of my Spirit will catch you up and carry you where I will. All that was will pass from you as you enter into the new day that is before you. I will justify you in the purposes of my Kingdom. I will restore you in the power of my anointing which will fulfill all that I have for you. We have a partnership that was formed before time began, and I am working everything together for the good of my people. Trust my leading as you follow in my footsteps! I will show you great and marvelous things that will take your breath away. I am establishing you on the high ground where you can watch my triumph pass before you. It is the time when I pour my new wine into fresh wineskins of my making. They will be pliant and flexible able to expand and grow as my Spirit carries out the will of the Righteous Father. His efforts will be multiplied on my behalf as you proceed in the direction I have planned for you. You will be amazed at what will be taking place. It will be like nothing remains the same and many changes will happen in the twinkling of an eye. You may start in one way only to discover I am leading you in a totally different direction. You will experience a depth of my love and intimacy in your worship of the Ancient of Days as never before known. You will see me high and lifted up before you as my presence fills the sanctuaries of my choosing. I will meet you face to face at the altar of my testimony. The atmosphere will be charged with an energy that will be life giving to all who receive it. A new sound from heaven will dominate your hearts with wonder and joy. Your eyes will be opened to see what I have prepared for my beloved in this time. The mantle of my righteousness will cover you from head to foot. It will be my doing, as you wait upon me with hopeful expectation!

Love,
JESUS

Habakkuk 2:2-3

²Then the LORD answered me and said: "Write the vision And make it plain on tablets, That he may run who reads it. ³For the vision is yet for an appointed time; But at the end it will speak, and it will not lie. Though it tarries, wait for it; Because it will surely come, It will not tarry."

Word Received March 28, 2002

You will sing a new song as my Spirit fills your heart with the wonder of my Kingdom. I will show you great and marvelous things as the days unfold before you. Trust in me and rely on my wisdom and grace! I will give you favor wherever and whenever you may need it. I have appropriated many things for you to carry out in my Name and for the honor of the Heavenly Father. You will be caught up in the fresh flow of my Spirit as he sweeps across the earth. The events around you will not hinder what I am doing with you. Proceed as my Spirit directs your steps and follow his leading! You will speak and act under his anointing, which will fulfill the will of the Father for you. Continue to worship the Ancient of Days with an honest and dedicated heart! Be at peace in me and experience the joy of your salvation even in the most trying of circumstances. Always remember that I am with you and my plans are for good and not for evil! Those I am partnering with you will come along side as committed friends for the long haul. You will be mutually blessed by what happens in your lives. The unity of my Holy Spirit is beginning to manifest in your gatherings where my Name is being lifted up. Your focus on my presence in worship will deepen and increase as your hearts are joined to mine. I have much to show you and I will bring it all to pass, as the time is ripe. Be still before me and hear what I am speaking to your heart! The wind of my Spirit is beginning to blow with a greater intensity, which will lift you higher into the mountaintop experiences of my glory. A golden cloud of my love and compassion will surround you. The old ways will be transformed into a whole new way of living for me. My joy will be your strength as you enter into the new day that is coming. Rest in me for I am with you!

Love,
JESUS

Psalm 67

¹God be merciful to us and bless us, And cause His face to shine upon us. Selah ²That Your way may be known on earth, Your salvation among all nations. ³Let the peoples praise You, O God; Let all the peoples praise You. ⁴Oh, let the nations be glad and sing for joy! For You shall judge the people righteously, And govern the nations on earth. Selah ⁵Let the peoples praise You, O God; Let all the peoples praise You. ⁶*Then the earth shall yield her increase; God, our own God, shall bless us.* ⁷*God shall bless us, And all the ends of the earth shall fear Him.*

Word Received March 29, 2002

The righteousness of my cross is followed by the triumph of my Resurrection. The victory has been won and my Holy Spirit is producing the fruit of it in your lives. I am calling you out into a new land of promise where my truth prevails. Your brokenness will be healed and your fortunes will be restored and added to. All that I have for you will be disclosed when I am ready to reveal it to you. Now trust and obey what I give you to do and say! I am releasing the fresh wind of my Spirit to blow through the land, destroying the strongholds of evil and setting my people free. The power of worship will be manifested among you as you enter into the true fellowship of my believers. You will experience a dimension of my love that has never before been seen on the earth. It is what I have been holding for you for this time. It will stamp out the grapes of wrath and release the joy of my salvation upon the earth. I will turn the hearts of many to me in these last days, and they will find the fulfillment of their hope in me. Continue on the road that I have set before you as it leads to the completion of my plans in your life! Your place in my Kingdom is assured as it is sealed in my blood by my Spirit in you. Always follow in the way of life that I have established for you! The anointing of my Spirit will carry you through to the ultimate conclusion of your calling in me. I am removing the distractions that have troubled your soul and I am renewing my presence within you. The goals I have set before you are hidden at times: for it is not necessary for you to know them for they are in my hands. Yield your heart and life to my Holy Spirit, for he will take you to new depths of intimacy with me! Heaven and earth will kiss in these moments that I have set apart for you. Enjoy them fully in the light of my glory!

Love,
JESUS

Hebrews 1:1-3
¹God, who at various times and in different ways spoke in time past to the fathers by the prophets, ²has in these last days spoken to us by His Son, whom He has appointed heir of all things, through whom also He made the worlds; ³who being the brightness of His glory and the express image of His person, and upholding all things by the word of His power, when He had by Himself purged our sins, sat down at the right hand of the Majesty on high,

Word Received March 30, 2002

I am releasing the sound of my triumphal song as you come crowding into my holy sanctuary. Worship the Ancient of Days with total abandon as my Resurrection power rises up within you! Surrender yourself—body, soul and spirit—to the outpouring of my Holy Spirit as you rise up to meet me in sweet communion! The lies of the enemy will lose their impact in the light of my truth being stirred up among you. Hearts and lives are being transformed as you declare my glory under the anointing of my Spirit. He will blow through like a tornado catching you up to the highest heaven. The new wine of my Spirit will intoxicate you with my love and affection. The wineskins that I have produced within you will expand and increase with my joy. You will be joined by the multitudes that come seeking my presence with you. I am making the connections that will last and bear much fruit in my Kingdom. There will be a joining and entwining of your hearts and lives with mine. Together we will march into the eternal dimensions that await you. The sincerity that I have placed in you will bond with those I have also touched with my mercy. The flow of my Holy Spirit will move you far beyond the limitations of your own minds and your own expectations. No eye has seen what I have prepared for you. My favor will be manifested wherever you find yourself in the days that lie before you. Everything has been for a purpose and you will see how it will all fit together in a true picture of the Father's plan for your life. Trust my will and allow it to have its way in you! Great and mighty events will be appearing on the earth as you take up my banner and follow me. My joy and gladness will be exploding in your midst as you meet with me in holy celebration. My Kingdom comes with love, joy and peace. Enjoy it forever!

Love,
JESUS

Romans 14:17-18
17 for the kingdom of God is not food and drink, but righteousness and peace and joy in the Holy Spirit. 18 For he who serves Christ in these things is acceptable to God and approved by men.

Word Received March 31, 2002

The new day of my righteousness has dawned and the light of my truth is being revealed. I am reaching out to touch you with a fresh vision from above. The trumpets are declaring the outpouring of my Spirit upon you. I will fill you with my love and joy: for this is the Resurrection glory manifested in you. Come and worship with the freedom I have won, for I am high and lifted up among you! The shattered dreams will be restored as my Spirit takes command of your destiny. Follow him to the mercy seat where we can be joined in an eternal embrace! The waterfall of my favor is being released for all to be soaked in my goodness. The healing of souls, and the renewing of lives once broken, will be like nothing you have ever seen. Come into the King's chamber and feast at the banquet I set before you. The wedding celebration has begun as my bride comes forth into her position. You are my beloved and all that I have is yours. My Kingdom is spread out before you as the multitudes come flocking into my holy sanctuary. There is a release of my Resurrection power that will totally dwarf anything ever known to man. It is the fulfillment of the hopes and longings of the ages. I am completing the connections and resolutions that the Righteous Father has planned from the beginning. All of the promises will find their satisfaction in me. I am the Alpha and the Omega, the beginning and end of all things. The crown of the universe is at my feet as I reign at the right hand of the Heavenly Father. Taste and see that my goodness and wonder will prevail forever and ever. The great cloud of witnesses has gathered around my throne and nations are awakening to my majesty. I will have my way upon the earth as it is in heaven for this is the will of the Ancient of Days. Now receive it for yourself!

Love,
JESUS

Philippians 2:5-11

⁵Let this mind be in you which was also in Christ Jesus, ⁶who, being in the form of God, did not consider it robbery to be equal with God, ⁷but made Himself of no reputation, taking the form of a servant, and coming in the likeness of men. ⁸And being found in appearance as a man, He humbled Himself and became obedient to the point of death, even the death of the cross. ⁹Therefore God also has highly exalted Him and given Him the name which is above every name, ¹⁰that at the name of Jesus every knee should bow, of those in heaven, and of those on earth, and of those under the earth, ¹¹and that every tongue should confess that Jesus Christ is Lord, to the glory of God the Father.

Word Received April 1, 2002

The overcoming power of my Resurrection is released *among* you by the unity of my Spirit *with* you. He is following through with everything that the Righteous Father has promised. He is bringing to pass all that has been planned for you from before time began. You are in the continuous flow from eternity to eternity. We are setting many things right and restoring a holy order to your life. It is all our doing from beginning to end. Trust our love for you and allow it to have its perfect work in your life! Receive what we give and celebrate our presence in your life. Worship with a fresh enthusiasm every time we meet together! Seek my face each day with a wholesome joy: for this is my desire for you! Approach the throne of the Ancient Days with an expectancy that overwhelms any of the negative things you may be feeling. I have established a path for you to follow and it leads to the fulfillment of who you are in me. Consider the challenges as opportunities for my favor to be manifested. Open doors await you as you proceed on the journey we have set before you. You do not travel alone, for I am with you and a great cloud of witnesses surrounds you. Many will be coming along side as you head for the common goal we have prepared for you. Daily we are renewing you by the impartation of my Spirit who lives in you. Wait upon me as loyal subjects of my eternal Kingdom: for I will show you the direction I have set for you. You are moving ahead even when it does not look like it. All things do work together for good in our hands, so trust and obey the leading we give you. Follow the inner prompting of my Holy Spirit in you and watch for the external confirmations! The seed of your prosperity have been sown and now comes the harvest of our Kingdom.

Love,
JESUS

Hebrews 12:1-2

[1]Therefore we also, since we are surrounded by so great a cloud of witnesses, let us lay aside every weight, and the sin which so easily ensnares us, and let us run with endurance the race that is set before us, [2]looking unto Jesus, the author and finisher of our faith, who for the joy that was set before Him endured the cross, despising the shame, and has sat down at the right hand of the throne of God.

Word Received April 2, 2002

I have heard your plea and I am answering with my gracious Word. Receive my blessing and let it fill your life with my goodness and joy! I will yet show you great and marvelous things as the days go by. All I have for you is far more than you can anticipate. My Kingdom truly appears with power and life for all who will turn to me, even in their moments of despair. I have overcome the world with all its defects and failures: for my victory is everlasting. Follow me into the tomorrow I have prepared for you and do not look back! I have set before you an open door that no one can shut. It leads to the place of promise that I have established for you. Again lean into the wind of my Holy

Spirit as it begins to blow from a new direction. Be prepared to go the way he is leading you. The times may be perilous but nothing escapes my notice. I have you in my hands and I will take you where I will and nothing will prevent you from going there. Seeds have been sown that have taken root and just now are bearing fruit. There is a great increase coming in every imaginable dimension. I am fulfilling the hopes and dreams of my people as the fears they have carried are removed. My truth will prevail and my Kingdom rule will be everywhere evident. Come into my presence and worship with a new found affection, for I am with you all the way! Trust my love for you and allow it to embrace you! Yes, the kisses of my mouth will seal our hearts forever. Cast your burdens upon me for I will bring them to a satisfying conclusion. Release yourself to me and hear the beating of my heart close to yours. It is a time of new beginnings and I hold them for you. Do not become anxious; only wait and see what I will be doing! Stand firm in what I have revealed to you, for my Spirit stands in it with you. Rejoice!

Love,
JESUS

Proverbs 21:21
²¹*He who follows righteousness and mercy finds life, righteousness and honor.*

Word Received April 3, 2002

The way of my truth is a river of life that carries you into my joy and gladness. The whole earth will be filled with my glory when my light has completely penetrated the darkness of people's hearts. I have set a time when it will all come together. I am challenging the lies that people have believed, and I am turning them around to my way of thinking. All I have for you will fill you with hope and peace as I put things in proper perspective for you. Trust my wisdom that I am placing in you by the revelation I am showing you! Rest in me and allow my Holy Spirit to guide you in what I give you. He knows the direction the Righteous Father has planned for you when he chose you from the beginning. Accept with honest and open appreciation those I have called to share with you in what I have purposed for you. They can be trusted, for they will stand with you, for they are of one mind with you. My Spirit will always give you the discernment of who they are, so you will not become anxious over it. Your bonding comes as you worship the Ancient of Days with hearts filled with my love. I am drawing you to me, and the closer you become, the more you are joined to one another. I have a purpose in it, which you cannot understand at this time. Just follow my leading and allow my Spirit to take charge of all that you are doing! There is much happening in the spiritual realm and some of it is beginning to appear in the natural. Wait and see what I have prepared for you! The outpouring of my Spirit is beginning again, with an even greater intensity that will transform even the hardest heart and mind. Rely on my judgment and do not try to second-guess what I am doing with you. The way before you is open; proceed as my Spirit directs you. Rejoice in the glory of my presence!

Love,
JESUS

Proverbs 3:5-6
⁵Trust in the LORD with all your heart, And lean not on your own understanding; ⁶In all your ways acknowledge Him, And He shall direct your paths.

Word Received April 4, 2002

My Word is life to your soul, as my Spirit moves in your heart my wonders to behold. My favor is upon you and I will make all things work together for my purposes. Trust me with everything that concerns you, and lay it all before me! I will take up your cause and carry it to a perfect solution according to my wisdom. All my plans are in place and they are being resolved one after another. Seek me in the quiet times and in the midst of the turmoil: for I am with you wherever you may be! Worship the Ancient of Days with a heartfelt fervor as my Spirit catches you up into heavenly of heavenlies! Proceed on the path that I have set before you, as my Spirit leads you for he knows the final outcome! I will prosper you far beyond anything you could imagine, for this is the will of the Heavenly Father. It will go far beyond material things, for they are only temporary. My Kingdom is eternal and the purposes of it are long-lasting and far-reaching. The impact of what I am doing in your life will touch many and will draw them to a deeper intimacy with me. The Resurrection power that I am releasing in you will bring healing and restoration to many who have been calling out to me. It is my strength and presence that will carry out my desires for them. The foundation of my love has been established in you and from it will grow a tree of life, which will bear much fruit to the glory of the Righteous Father. Your roots have sunk deep in me through the trials and challenges you have encountered. Count it all joy, for it has been the decisions we have made in your life! Follow as my Spirit guides you into the tomorrow that lies before you. The world does not see what you see, for it is discerned by a believing heart. Rely on me for your direction and for the ability to carry out what I show you! It is time to go forward!

Love,
JESUS

Zephaniah 3:17

17The LORD your God in your midst, The Mighty One, will save; He will rejoice over you with gladness, He will quiet you with His love, He will rejoice over you with singing."

Word Received April 5, 2002

The focus of my righteousness is your joy and gladness. Proceed on to the next stage that I have prepared for you! Yesterday is over and tomorrow is yet to begin. Follow in the path I have established for you, and enjoy the journey I have given you. All that I have for you will come together at the proper time. Saturate yourself in my presence as I pour out my kindness upon you. Worship with a tender heart and an expectant spirit! Rejoice in my victory and let it carry you to new heights in me! Set aside the old ways of thinking and be challenged by the fresh opportunities I am bringing to you. All that I have for you is far greater than anything you could imagine even in your fondest dreams. Things will be happening very quickly for you, and I will be putting together some very wonderful things. Wait upon me and let my patience permeate your being! Take hold of what I place in your hands and appreciate what I give you. Continually sow my truth wherever you are and watch it take root miraculously in those who receive it! You will see the fruit appear in exponential amounts. It will trigger even greater returns for my Kingdom. Set your heart and mind on what is above where my glory dwells! Let it flood your soul and transform your experiences. All of it rests in my hands as I take you to a new level of intimacy with me. My kisses will be upon your lips as heaven and earth touch in my fondest embrace. I am calling to you to come up higher into the place I have prepared for you. I am surrounding you with those who are diligently following in my footsteps. I am binding you together in my love and compassion. Sights and sounds will change as you lift up my Name in your midst. The heavens will shower down the signs and wonders of my mercy. It is a time for celebration!

Love,
JESUS

Haggai 2:6-9

⁶"For thus says the LORD of hosts: 'Once more (it is a little while) I will shake heaven and earth, the sea and dry land; ⁷and I will shake all nations, and they shall come to the Desire of All Nations, and I will fill this temple with glory,' says the LORD of hosts. ⁸'The silver is Mine, and the gold is Mine,' says the LORD of hosts. ⁹'The glory of this latter temple shall be greater than the former,' says the LORD of hosts. 'And in this place I will give peace,' says the LORD of hosts."

Word Received April 6, 2002

The fire of my glory will transform all it touches. Nothing remains the same after you have experienced the fullness of my presence. I am showering down my goodness and mercy even in the most bizarre circumstances. I am overriding what was meant for evil and turning it to my purposes. All that is happening will reflect my hand in it. Trust my love and my wisdom for I will bring a sudden change of events in my direction! Continue in the revelation I have given and allow my truth to set the captives free! There will be a spiraling upward as you are caught in the wind of my Spirit, as he carries you beyond your limitations. It is in the times of worship that you will see most clearly into the realm of my Spirit. Yield to it and follow it as it takes you even beyond belief. The river of life is rising among you to restore you in my good graces. I am exposing and silencing the lies of the evil one, for he will not come near your dwelling in me. I am saturating you in my love and compassion as you lead others to me. I will fulfill the destiny I have for you and nothing will be able to stop it. I am encompassing my people in my embrace as I carry them within my heart. I have established you on the high ground and my victory is assured. Follow the leading of my Holy Spirit as he takes you where no one has gone before. You are entering a new phase of the Righteous Father's plan for you. It will bring you into a reality of wonder never before seen on the earth. I will bring many with you as you truly experience the touch of my hand upon you. I have set the times and the places when heaven and earth will be joined by my presence with you. There will be an increased bonding of hearts and lives as you are together with me. I have opened the door that cannot be shut; so enter in with a joyful heart!

Love,
JESUS

Ephesians 1:3-10

³Blessed be the God and Father of our Lord Jesus Christ, who has blessed us with every spiritual blessing in the heavenly places in Christ, ⁴just as He chose us in Him before the foundation of the world, that we should be holy and without blame before Him in love, ⁵having predestined us to adoption as sons by Jesus Christ to Himself, according to the good pleasure of His will, ⁶to the praise of the glory of His grace, by which He made us accepted in the Beloved. ⁷In Him we have redemption through His blood, the forgiveness of sins, according to the riches of His grace ⁸which He made to abound toward us in all wisdom and prudence, ⁹having made known to us the mystery of His will, according to His good pleasure which He purposed in Himself, ¹⁰that in the dispensation of the fullness of the times He might gather together in one all things in Christ, both which are in heaven and which are on earth—in Him.

Word Received April 7, 2002

Worship the Righteous Father in the beauty of my holiness that is being poured out upon you! You are my people, called by my Name, and I rejoice over you with singing. My presence is with you and I fill you with the power of my Spirit. My anointing destroys the yokes of bondage and releases the fragrance of your love. It is in faithfulness that my favor abounds and my joy is released. I have sealed you in my Holy Spirit and he is the strength of your convictions. He supplies all your needs and guides your steps. His wisdom brings forth the truth of my revelation in all that you do and say. His peace determines your position before me. He transforms what could have been a disaster into an overwhelming victory. Trust his voice within you and the boldness he speaks through you! Come and join in my celebration of the new day that has dawned! Worship with the abandon of one who knows me in the fullness of our intimacy together! Let go of yourselves and throw yourself into my arms as a bride goes to her beloved! Sing, shout and dance before me with gladness as my glory comes down to envelop you in the cloud of my righteousness! Heaven is breaking through as the dividing veil has been torn apart for you. I come in the fullness of my Holy Spirit to impart life as I restore you to myself. The enemy is under your feet, for my triumph has put him there. The sounds of the trumpets ring true as they herald my presence among you. I am with you, my wonders to perform and my healing to bestow. It is freedom that I bring, as the gates of hell wither at my glance. My Resurrection has released more than you have realized. It is my Kingdom that has come to be established in the hearts of those I have touched. I rule and reign in love, for I am the King of kings! Come and enter in!

Love,
JESUS

John 4:23-24

23But the hour is coming, and now is, when the true worshipers will worship the Father in spirit and truth; for the Father is seeking such to worship Him. 24God is Spirit, and those who worship Him must worship in spirit and truth."

Word Received April 9, 2002

What has been hidden will be disclosed, all to my glory and purpose. Trust in my goodness in all of it! Follow the leading of my Holy Spirit and allow him to take you where he wills. He will show you what to do and say in every circumstance. He will set your priorities and he will make them work. The wind has quickened as the time draws near for my will to be done on the earth. There is more at stake than you realize, but do not fear, for I have overcome. I am carrying out the plans of the Righteous Father in your life. Always seek me first in prayer and reflection! Remember, I am the beginning and the end of everything that exists! My authority overrides all others and I have placed my anointing upon you. Be at peace in it for it will cover all that you do! There is a shaking going on, so my truth will be revealed in all of its fullness. The seed has been sown and now is the time of harvest so proceed accordingly! Set your sights higher and aim further than you have ever done. There are still greater things coming and the enemy has sought to distract you. Enter again the flow of my Spirit for he will bring you to the appropriate results! Come and worship as a royal priesthood, a holy nation, a people after my own heart! Lift up my Name and honor the Ancient of Days! Blow the trumpet in Zion and see the walls of oppression fall before you! I am gathering my people from where they have been scattered by unbelief and doubt. I am restoring them to their rightful place in me. See the plans I have for you and know that they are good and they will bear much fruit! Be open to what I am showing you and follow it to the ultimate conclusion! Hear what my Spirit is speaking for this time and declare it before the nations! There is a radical transformation coming and you have a part in it.

Love,
JESUS

Zechariah 2:10-11

[10]"Sing and rejoice, O daughter of Zion! For behold, I am coming and I will dwell in your midst," says the LORD. [11]"Many nations shall be joined to the LORD in that day, and they shall become My people. And I will dwell in your midst. Then you will know that the LORD of hosts has sent Me to you."

Word Received April 10, 2002

I have truly opened the door that no one can shut and I am following through on everything I have planned. Trust my judgment and let my Spirit take you where I want you to go! I will satisfy all your needs and I will provide everything that is necessary for you. Enter into a time of daily worship with me even if it is only on the inside. We are joined together by my Spirit who dwells there in you. When the moments come to release it all with those I have brought to you, enjoy it all with even greater fervor! It is a time for uniting in the wonders of my Kingdom. My Spirit hovers over the seeming chaos and he will bring a new creation out of it. I am breaking through the hard crust of reality into the warmth and joy that lies hidden beneath. I am saturating you with my anointing, which is carrying out my purposes in your life. It is not always seen on the surface, for much of it is going on beneath, where I am working, too. Each day has an opportunity that was not there the day before, so grab a hold of it! Push through until you experience the fullness of my presence with you! I will remove the discouragement, and give you a hope and expectation that cannot be quenched. Proceed on the journey I have set before you and know that nothing remains the same in my Kingdom! The challenges will come, but be of good cheer for I have overcome the world. The sights and sounds of the conflict that rages are the birth pangs of the new day I have promised. Be alert to what my Spirit is speaking into existence in your life! Let him draw aside the veil from what I have in store for you! The joyful times will come when you least expect them. They will flow from your relationship with me. Come and enter into the fruitfulness that I am producing in your life by my Spirit! It is there for you!

Love,
JESUS

Zechariah 4:6

⁶So he answered and said to me: "This is the word of the LORD to Zerubbabel: Not by might nor by power, but by My Spirit,' Says the LORD of hosts."

Word Received April 11, 2002

The wave of my Spirit is coming and it will carry you further than you have ever been. It will wash away the obstacles to my will being done in you and around you. My Kingdom will produce the fruit of righteousness as my purposes are being fulfilled. Rest in the assurance that all things will work together for the good that I have determined! Open gates will greet you as you proceed along the path that I have set for you. Words of knowledge and wisdom will flow from your lips as my Spirit speaks through you. Appropriate for yourself what I have prepared for you, and do not disdain the small beginnings! Each step leads you closer to the completion I have for you. You are part of the plan that the Heavenly Father has formulated for this time. It will produce countless victories in every area for all my people. Approach my throne of grace with an open and accepting heart, for you are most welcome there! Come into my presence with thanksgiving and praise, worshipping the Ancient of Days with all of the love that is in you! It is my good pleasure to give you the Kingdom with all its wonder and joy.

I will separate the sheep from the goats at the appropriate time, and it is of no concern to you. I will do it! Continue in the flow of my Holy Spirit, for that is your destiny! It was so from before the beginning as I chose you for partnership with me in my Kingdom. There are many others who are yet to come in, and they, too, will find their place in me. Trust my love and do not lean on your own understanding! I am leading you and I am supporting you. I am joining you to those I have called to be alongside of you in the mission that you share together. Today you will see openings that you never knew were there, and my Spirit will enable you to take advantage of them. Rejoice!

Love,
JESUS

Zechariah 4:14

[14]*So he said, "These are the two anointed ones, who stand beside the Lord of the whole earth."*

Word Received April 12, 2002

My anointing is restoring the edge to the sword of my Spirit in your life. It is the oil that flows from the heavenly lamp stands that burns brightly in your soul. It draws the righteous to join with you in the task that I place before you. I am gathering those I have called to enter into a covenant with you under my direction and persuasion. It is my Kingdom heritage that is producing in you the worshipping desire for the Ancient of Days. It is the wind of my Spirit that is sweeping you into the radical transformations that are coming upon you. It is the new day that has never been seen until now. It is an outpouring revelation of my Resurrection power that heralds the final days of my creation. You are to stand on the ramparts and see the glory of my presence transpiring before you. Time will stand still and accelerate at the same time. It is the wheel within the wheel that will push you forward into the tomorrow that was prophesied yesterday. Changes will follow changes in rapid succession. All will be within the parameters I have established for your life. Joy and gladness will flood your soul as the freedom I have won for you is released in you. You will turn over new leaves in your life as the events of these last days unfold before you. Take heart, for it is all the will of the Righteous Father who deeply loves you! The multitudes will let go of the old ways and come seeking after me. They will encounter my Spirit in the middle of what is occurring in their lives. You will celebrate together in the watershed experience of the new life that is being born afresh in you. It will be received and believed without explanation. All this awaits you as you turn the next corner of your life. Step through the open door that is before you and enter into the fullness of your salvation!

Love,
JESUS

Revelation 19:1-10

[1]After these things I heard a loud voice of a great multitude in heaven, saying, "Alleluia! Salvation and glory and honor and power to the Lord our God! [2]For true and righteous are His judgments, because He has judged the great harlot who corrupted the earth with her fornication; and He has avenged on her the blood of His servants shed by her." [3]Again they said, "Alleluia! Her smoke rises up forever and ever!" [4]And the twenty-four elders and the four living creatures fell down and worshiped God who sat on the throne, saying, "Amen! Alleluia!" [5]Then a voice came from the throne, saying, "Praise our God, all you His servants and those who fear Him, both small and great!" [6]And I heard, as it were, the voice of a great multitude, as the sound of many waters and as the sound of mighty thunderings, saying, "Alleluia! For the Lord God Omnipotent reigns! [7]Let us be glad and rejoice and give Him glory, for the marriage of the Lamb has come, and His wife has made herself ready." [8]And to her it was granted to be arrayed in fine linen, clean and bright, for the fine linen is the righteous acts of the saints. [9]Then he said to me, "Write: 'Blessed are those who are called to the marriage supper of the Lamb!'" And he said to me, "These are the true sayings of God." [10]And I fell at his feet to worship him. But he said to me, "See that you do not do that! I am your fellow servant, and of your brethren who have the testimony of Jesus. Worship God! For the testimony of Jesus is the spirit of prophecy."

Word Received April 13, 2002

Strike out in the new direction I am giving you! Follow my Holy Spirit into the arena of your dreams where I have called you! Signs and wonders await you there as the fullness of my presence is manifested in all that will be taking place. Proceed according to my will as my Holy Spirit reveals it to you as he gathers everything together for you! Each opportunity is an open door into another room of the house that I am building where my glory dwells. I am partnering you with many who have come through the fire of purification and tempering. They are like perfectly formed steel blades to be wielded by my Spirit in the events that lay ahead of you. Transparent hearts, filled with my love, will transform those they touch at the deepest levels of their existence. Place your hand in mine and I will lead you to the position I have established for you! I will crown your efforts with success as you move forward in my Name. You will encounter me in the depths of your being as you worship the Righteous Father by my Spirit and in my truth. Receive your manifest destiny as my glory surrounds you and carries you into the throne room of heaven, where I stand at the right hand of the Ancient of Days! All the earth is spread before me and my purposes are being carried out there. The eyes of the blind will be opened and the chains of the oppressed will be removed. Bodies and souls will be healed of there infirmities as the wings of my Spirit passes over them. The trumpets will sound again and again as my Kingdom comes in the fullness of power in the hearts of those who have received me. I am going before you to prepare the place for you of my own choosing. It will be filled with peace and joy as you gather together with those I have called for such a time as this. Watch and wait upon me!

Love,
JESUS

Psalm 84

¹How lovely is Your tabernacle, O LORD of hosts! ²My soul longs, yes, even faints For the courts of the LORD; My heart and my flesh cry out for the living God. ³Even the sparrow has found a home, And the swallow a nest for herself, Where she may lay her young—Even Your altars, O LORD of hosts, My King and my God. ⁴Blessed are those who dwell in Your house; They will still be praising You. Selah ⁵Blessed is the man whose strength is in You, Whose heart is set on pilgrimage. ⁶As they pass through the Valley of Baca, They make it a spring; The rain also covers it with pools. They go from strength to strength; Each one appears before God in Zion. ⁸O LORD God of hosts, hear my prayer; Give ear, O God of Jacob! Selah ⁹O God, behold our shield, And look upon the face of Your anointed. ¹⁰For a day in Your courts is better than a thousand. I would rather be a doorkeeper in the house of my God Than dwell in the tents of wickedness. ¹¹For the LORD God is a sun and shield; The LORD will give grace and glory; No good thing will He withhold From those who walk uprightly. ¹²O LORD of hosts, Blessed is the man who trusts in You!

Word Received April 14, 2002

The fire of my holiness will descend upon you like a cloud to cover your nakedness. It will transform you into the image that I have created you to be. You will reflect my glory for all to see, and be drawn into the circle of my arms. I have placed you upon the mountaintop where you can soar like eagles in my presence. The gentleness of my Spirit will be like a dove resting upon you. My light will flood your gatherings as you worship in my Spirit and in the truth of my love. The challenges of the moment will be replaced by my victory from above. Everything will be changed in the twinkling of an eye as my Resurrection power is released among you. The walls and barriers will be broken and my rule will be established for all time. The sovereign will of the Ancient of Days will prevail as you pass through the veil of tears into my eternal joy. I am releasing you to experience what I have been holding for you in this time. My salvation will do a complete work in you, healing and restoring you to one mind with me. You will be exposed to revelation after revelation coming from the Righteous Father as he watches over you. Signs and wonders will confirm what you will be hearing and seeing through my Spirit. Act and speak only as my Spirit directs you for he alone knows all that I am doing in these last days! Continually bow before the Gracious Father who loves you as you pray and worship before me! The wind of my Spirit is about to explode in your midst bringing to fruition all that I have intended for this time. Seek me beyond your needs and blessings for I know them all! I hold you in my hand and I will not let you go. I am building my house on the solid rock of my truth revealed by my Spirit. There is a new sound coming which will penetrate your inner most being. It is the voice of heaven.

Love,
JESUS

Psalm 85

¹LORD, You have been favorable to Your land; You have brought back the captivity of Jacob. ²You have forgiven the iniquity of Your people; You have covered all their sin. Selah. ³You have taken away all Your wrath; You have turned from the fierceness of Your anger. ⁴Restore us, O God of our salvation, And cause Your anger toward us to cease. ⁵Will You be angry with us forever? Will You prolong Your anger to all generations? ⁶Will You not revive us again, That Your people may rejoice in You? ⁷Show us Your mercy, LORD, And grant us Your salvation. ⁸I will hear what God the LORD will speak, For He will speak peace To His people and to His saints; But let them not turn back to folly. ⁹Surely His salvation is near to those who fear Him, That glory may dwell in our land. ¹⁰Mercy and truth have met together; Righteousness and peace have kissed. ¹¹Truth shall spring out of the earth, And righteousness shall look down from heaven. ¹²Yes, the LORD will give what is good; And our land will yield its increase. ¹³Righteousness will go before Him, And shall make His footsteps our pathway.

Word Received April 15, 2002

My truth remains after everything else has fallen away. I am with you and my will is being done. Trust my love for you as you continue your journey with me. I am opening the doors for you and I am leading you through them. We are traveling together into the new day of my promise for you. There is much that is taking place and it is all serving my purposes. Many things may be hidden, but not to me. I also see the end from the beginning. Let my Holy Spirit take you where he wills for he alone knows the destination I have for you. Each day will be filled with my blessings for you. It is up to you to recognize them when they come. Some may be disguised, but they are still there. Proceed with what I give you and allow it to take its course! You will be moving beyond your capabilities, so you will need to depend upon me for your wisdom and strength. I will neither disappoint you nor forsake you. It is a holy mission that you are on, configured to the desires of the Righteous Father who loves you personally. It is all part of his greater plan that is being worked out on the earth. Come now and worship at his feet and enjoy his favor forever! There are connections being made, which will serve for the moment, and then there are some that will have lasting meaning for you. I will show you the difference when it is necessary for you to know it. Always remember that I am the friend who is closer than a brother! I will always complement your efforts with the success that I bring to all my relationships. Rest in me and watch what I have in store for you! Many things are coming together as my Kingdom comes in power and light to you. I have established you on the firm foundation of my calling, which will always be there. Look ahead and see me moving before you as I set things in place for you!

Love,
JESUS

Psalm 87

¹His foundation is in the holy mountains. ²The LORD loves the gates of Zion More than all the dwellings of Jacob. ³Glorious things are spoken of you, O city of God! Selah. ⁴"I will make mention of Rahab and Babylon to those who know Me; Behold, O Philistia and Tyre, with Ethiopia: This one was born there.'" ⁵And of Zion it will be said, "This one and that one were born in her; And the Most High Himself shall establish her." ⁶The LORD will record, When He registers the peoples: "This one was born there." Selah ⁷Both the singers and the players on instruments say, "All my springs are in you."

Word Received April 16, 2002

The flight of the eagles has begun as I bring them to their nesting places. I am restoring them in the fulfillment of my promises. I am partnering them according to my plans. Everything will be accomplished, as I desire it to be. You are being strengthened by the fresh visions I have for you. I will show you great and mighty things as the time progresses. Continue to pray as I lead you, for many doors are being opened to you. Proceed along the path that is before you, for it is the one of my choosing! Sow the seed of my truth in all that you do and with all that you touch. I have placed my integrity in you. Allow my Spirit to bring you to those moments of worship and exultation in my Name, for it is there that we are joined together. There is a process of transformation going on as I build my people into a cohesive organism directed by my Spirit. Your place in it is assured from the beginning and you will reap the benefits as well. Guard your heart for it is always vulnerable, for it is the center of your being. Welcome those I send to be connected with you and I will build the relationship you should have with them! Love is a feeling as well as an action and both are under my protection. I will show you what to do with them. Take the time to be with me so I can show you what is coming next in your life. Always seek my face in all matters, and leave the rest in my hands, for I know the plans I have for them. I am restoring your confidence in me, and I am sharpening the edge of your sword. Be at peace and watch what I will be doing in the days ahead. Sound the trumpets and follow my leading! All that has gone before was only a foretaste of the wonders that are coming. I am realigning my forces for the final outcome of my plans. Take time to enjoy what I am doing!

Love,
JESUS

Psalm 89:1-2
1 I will sing of the mercies of the LORD forever; With my mouth will I make known Your faithfulness to all generations. 2 For I have said, "Mercy shall be built up forever; Your faithfulness You shall establish in the very heavens."

Word Received April 17, 2002

It is a time of new beginnings as my people follow after me. I am bringing things together that could not be possible before this time. Follow the leading of my Holy Spirit as he speaks within and confirms it in what is taking place. Stretch your mind and heart beyond the ordinary. See with my eyes and know with my heart for I am bringing the greater things into being for you! I am establishing my people in the center of the turmoil that is going on. There will be times when you stand upon the mountain watching what is taking place before you. There will be moments when you will be deeply involved in what will be occurring. In either case it will be my will for you. Trust my wisdom and be open to what I am doing with you! The false prophets are losing their hold and my truth is triumphing. The lies are being exposed for what they are and will be of no effect. Come into my presence where we can enjoy sweet communion together! Worship the Heavenly Father with your newfound joy and enthusiasm! His love watches over you and my Spirit guides your every step. There is much to come in every form of your existence. Relationships will blossom and finances will prosper as you enter into the fullness of my Kingdom. The era of want is coming to an end. Blessings will follow you as you take the road that I have laid out for you. It is not a matter of your understanding but of my mercy. Show yourself approved as you allow me to take charge of all that I have for you. It is a time to shout and leap for joy as my glory covers you with the mantle of my presence. Speak and act under the anointing of my authority! Do not shrink back, but lunge ahead into the tomorrow that I set before you. I am building partnerships that will have lasting significance in your life. Receive them gladly!

Love,
JESUS

Psalm 90:14
[14]*Oh, satisfy us early with Your mercy, That we may rejoice and be glad all our days!*

Word Received April 18, 2002

There is a sound coming from the highest heaven, which will reach every corner of the earth. It will radically transform everything that is happening. It will restore my purposes as it reaches into the heart of everyone who hears it. You will take a turn in a new direction, which will lead you to the outcome that I have prepared for you. I will challenge the opposition to my plans and overcome them. I am finalizing what I have begun in you so you can take your rightful place with me. My eagles will catch the fresh wind of my Spirit and soar to new heights in me. Healing of body, soul and spirit will become a natural part of what my Kingdom brings. I am separating you to myself, and there will be no one else who can come between us. I am drawing you into my secret place where I can pour my wisdom and love into you. I will prosper what is happening on the outside as I restore you on the inside. My peace will stand as a protection over you as you move according to my will. Those that you have trusted because of me will not desert you in your time of need. They have become true partners in my Kingdom work. Some may fall away but that is to be expected given the nature of humanity. You are going to a deeper level of worship and reflection where we are joined together. I will be with you in the night watches and in the dawning of the new day. I will go before you to make the crooked ways straight and the rough places smooth. It will reflect what I am doing with you in these last days. There will be a harmony in my Holy Spirit that will bring phenomenal results in my growing Kingdom among you. Depart from the norm and enter into the signs and wonders that I am doing! All that has happened will work for my good. Do not resist it, but be joined to it!

Love,
JESUS

Psalm 91

[1] *He who dwells in the secret place of the Most High Shall abide under the shadow of the Almighty.* [2] *I will say of the LORD, "He is my refuge and my fortress; My God, in Him I will trust."* [3] *Surely He shall deliver you from the snare of the fowler And from the perilous pestilence.* [4] *He shall cover you with His feathers, And under His wings you shall take*

refuge; His truth shall be your shield and buckler. ⁵You shall not be afraid of the terror by night, Nor of the arrow that flies by day, ⁶Nor of the pestilence that walks in darkness, Nor of the destruction that lays waste at noonday. ⁷A thousand may fall at your side, And ten thousand at your right hand; But it shall not come near you. ⁸Only with your eyes shall you look, And see the reward of the wicked. ⁹Because you have made the LORD, who is my refuge, Even the Most High, your habitation place, ¹⁰No evil shall befall you, Nor shall any plague come near your dwelling; ¹¹For He shall give His angels charge over you, To keep you in all your ways. ¹²In their hands they shall bear you up, Lest you dash your foot against a stone. ¹³You shall tread upon the lion and the cobra, The young lion and the serpent you shall trample underfoot. ¹⁴"Because he has set his love upon Me, therefore I will deliver him; I will set him on high, because he has known My name. ¹⁵He shall call upon Me, and I will answer him; I will be with him in trouble; I will deliver him and honor him. ¹⁶With long life I will satisfy him, And show him My salvation."

Word Received April 19, 2002

The clouds are parting and the sunshine of my face is beaming through to you. My favor and grace are with you. Enjoy what I am doing with you! Place your trust in me, for everything that concerns you is ultimately in my hands! Come again into the flow of my Spirit as he captures your imagination with the greater things that are coming. Worship the Ancient of Days with a sincere and committed heart for he is worthy! Show yourself approved as you diligently take hold of what my Spirit is revealing to you! His anointing is upon you endowing you with capabilities that are far beyond the norm. He is also piecing many things together to give you a more complete picture of what has been going on. He will confirm everything he has for you with signs and wonders following, as you enter into them. Walk through what he is speaking to your inner person! He is removing the cobwebs of old thinking and replacing it with bold insight. Step out beyond what you normally would do as my Spirit grabs a hold of you! He is catching you up in a whirlwind that will take you far into the future I have prepared for you. Seeds long sown are now bearing much fruit that is adding wholeheartedly to my harvest. Much of it was sown in secret and far beyond your comprehension. It was the hidden work of my Holy Spirit carrying out the will of the Righteous Father. You will be reaping the results in many and unusual ways. Give honor and praise to whom it is due and proceed with what I have for you! Sincerity of heart far outshines glibness of tongue. You will be faithful as I am faithful: for you are my beloved. All the days of your life are in my hand and I am with you forever. Trumpets will sound calling the faithful to gather in my Name. They will come crowding into the places I have provided!

Love,
JESUS

Psalm 92

¹It is good to give thanks to the LORD, And to sing praises to Your name, O Most High; ²To declare Your lovingkindness in the morning, And Your faithfulness every night, ³On an instrument of ten strings, On the lute, And on the harp, With harmonious sound. ⁴For You, LORD, have made me glad through Your work; I will triumph in the works of Your hands. ⁵O LORD, how great are Your works! Your thoughts are very deep. ⁶A senseless man does not know, Nor does a fool understand this. ⁷When the wicked spring up like grass, And when all the workers of iniquity flourish, It is that they may be destroyed forever. ⁸But You, LORD, are on high forevermore. ⁹For behold, Your enemies, O LORD, For behold, Your enemies shall perish; All the workers of iniquity shall be scattered. ¹⁰But my horn You have exalted like a wild ox; I have been anointed with fresh oil. ¹¹My eye also has seen my desire on my enemies; My ears hear my desire on the wicked Who rise up against me. ¹²The righteous shall flourish like a palm tree, He shall grow like a cedar in Lebanon. ¹³Those who are planted in the house of the LORD Shall flourish in the courts of our God. ¹⁴They shall still bear fruit in old age; They shall be fresh and flourishing, ¹⁵To declare that the LORD is upright; He is my rock, and there is no unrighteousness in Him.

Word Received April 20, 2002

The eagles are flying to their designated locations where they will carry out what I have called them to do. Only those who trust in me with all their hearts will fully see what I have in store for them. Approach my throne of grace with an open heart and a willing spirit! I will not let you be distracted from the course I have set for your life. There will be things happening that you do not understand, but in the end I will have the will of the Father done in all situations. Proceed as I lead you, and, again, do not look to the right or the left but straight ahead before you! Search out my wisdom in all circumstances and listen for my voice in your inward parts! The enemy has sought to sift you, but his hand can no longer interfere with what I am doing. I am setting the captives free and I am bringing them into what I have prepared for them. I am increasing the depth and quality of your devotion to me, as you worship the Heavenly Father with a sincere heart. Come into my presence with thanksgiving and praise … leaving everything else outside! The wounds will be healed as you focus your attention on the fulfillment of my Kingdom among you. I am saturating you with my Spirit as he brings you to new dimensions in our relationship with each other. No one will ever come between us, for we are joined together forever. Partnerships on earth will come and go as they serve my purposes for the furtherance of my Kingdom. What I am doing now will have far deeper consequences than you could ever realize. Rest in my peace and let my Spirit carry you today! Be aware of what is going on around you but do not be influenced by it! My plans are going forward for what I have intended for you from the beginning. I will prosper you in many and varied ways all for the glory of my Kingdom!

Love,
JESUS

Psalm 93

¹The LORD reigns, He is clothed with majesty; The LORD is clothed, He has girded Himself with strength. Surely the world is established, so that it cannot be moved. ²Your throne is established from of old; You are from everlasting. ³The floods have lifted up, O LORD, The floods have lifted up their voice; The floods lift up their waves. ⁴The

LORD on high is mightier Than the noise of many waters, Than the mighty waves of the sea. ⁵Your testimonies are very sure; Holiness adorns Your house, O LORD, forever.

Word Received April 21, 2002

It is done, it is done the victory is won and you are complete in me! Trust my Spirit to bring everything to a firm conclusion in me! I am heralding the new day when everything will come together in perfect harmony. All that has been expected will come to fruition in your life. Partners in my Good News will rise up in every place to declare my glory for all to see. Come into my presence now and experience my joy everlasting: for my day has dawned for all to receive with great enthusiasm. I am breaking you loose from the bondage of the past as I reveal the hope that lies before you. Worship in the triumph that I am pouring out upon you! You will fly with eagles' wings into the upper reaches of my Kingdom where the light shines brightest. You will be caught up in a whirlwind as my Spirit scoops you up into the heavenly throne room. All of this is only a prelude to the radical awakening that is coming upon the earth. The towers have fallen to make way for the magnificence of the edifice of my majesty being raised up. Sights and sounds will intensify as my Spirit floods the land with my truth. The defeat of the forces of darkness is complete, and now comes the deliverance of those who were held in captivity to them. Oceans of grace will cover the land and the harvest will begin. Your eyes will see what I have planned as my mantle of authority rests upon you. The anointing that is being released on you will accomplish mighty works in my Name. The healing revolution has begun in the fulfillment of my promises. You will see the lame walk, the blind see and the dead raised up in me. Your faithfulness will be rewarded by the greater things that will be revealed through you. The birth pangs are over and the delivery has come. It is the new day in which the Father's will is being accomplished!

Love,
JESUS

Colossians 2:6-15

[6]As you therefore have received Christ Jesus the Lord, so walk in Him, [7]rooted and built up in Him and established in the faith, as you have been taught, abounding in it with thanksgiving. [8]Beware lest anyone cheat you through philosophy and empty deceit, according to the tradition of men, according to the basic principles of the world, and not according to Christ. [9]For in Him dwells all the fullness of the Godhead bodily; [10]and you are complete in Him, who is the head of all principality and power. [11]In Him you were also circumcised with the circumcision made without hands, by putting off the body of the sins of the flesh, by the circumcision of Christ, [12]buried with Him in baptism, in which you also were raised with Him through faith in the working of God, who raised Him from the dead. [13]And you, being dead in your trespasses and the uncircumcision of your flesh, He has made alive together with Him, having forgiven you all trespasses, [14]having wiped out the handwriting of requirements that was against us, which was contrary to us. And He has taken it out of the way, having nailed it to the cross. [15]Having disarmed principalities and powers, He made a public spectacle of them, triumphing over them in it.

Word Received April 22, 2002

The latter rain of my Spirit is releasing the sweet fragrance of my presence among you. It falls on the just and the unjust alike so that some may be saved. My Spirit has established my work in you that is bearing fruit in the most unusual ways. You will be amazed at what will be taking place as you continue on your journey with me. There will be deep moments of intimacy … as you feel my lips touching you and my arms embracing you with my love. You will never again be alone for I am with you always. There will also be wild and exciting moments as the intensity of my worship bursts forth within you. You will dance before your King who rejoices over you with singing and pours out his blessings upon you. I will be drawing you into closer relationships with those who have caught my vision of things to come. You will be a force to be reckoned with as you pursue the purposes I have set for you. My Kingdom is revealed in truth and power, which transforms lives. Walk in it without fear or compromise! Receive it all in the very depth of your being! I have chosen you to bear fruit that remains fresh and alive. You belong to me and nothing can take you from me. I have placed the seal of my Holy Spirit upon you as my holy treasure. There are changes coming that will confirm what I have been promising you from the beginning. Your hope has not been in vain, for it will be played out in the days ahead of you. Trust me and rest in my peace, which I give to you! Lay down your burdens—and the burdens that others seek to put upon you—for neither are productive. I will carry them to a successful outcome. Now enter into the joy that I have prepared for you. Experience the comfort and strength that I am pouring out upon you! All things will work together for my glory and your blessing!

Love,
JESUS

Song of Solomon 1:2-4

²Let him kiss me with the kisses of his mouth—For your love is better than wine. ³Because of the fragrance of your good ointments, Your name is ointment poured forth; Therefore the virgins love you. ⁴Draw me away! We will run after you. The king has brought me into his chambers. We will be glad and rejoice in you. We will remember your love more than wine. Rightly do they love you.

Word Received April 23, 2002

The doors are open and my glory is shining through ... for you and for all who are following me. I have placed in your hand the sword of triumph, which will set the captives free and accomplish the greater works that I have promised. All things will begin to come together according to my plan and timing. Shattered dreams will be healed as the higher purposes I have in store for you come into play. All things are under my will and authority, for I am accomplishing the will of the Righteous Father. My Holy Spirit is carrying them out for the advancement of my Kingdom among you. Today, receive what I am giving to you as a precious gift from my heart to yours! I will show you mighty things cloaked in the disguise of the insignificant. Minor details will carry major impact as they are being worked out. I am forming my character in everyone who yields to my love. Enter into your worship of the Ancient of Days with great expectations for what will be happening there! Heaven and earth are joined in those moments as the cloud of my presence surrounds you. I am drawing and leading you into the positions I have established for you. They are far and above anything you may have ever imagined. Their impact on my people will be increased exponentially as the ripples spread far and wide. You will catch the wave of my Spirit that is breaking upon the earth, and it will carry you further than you have ever come before in the realm of my Spirit. You will be experiencing an even greater freedom in all that you will be accomplishing in my Name. You will see old wounds closed up instantaneously as my Spirit is released more and more. Trust my wisdom and discernment as you allow me to speak my truth to each situation that comes to you! My authority and anointing rests upon you. Rejoice in it!

Love,
JESUS

Psalm 95

¹Oh come, let us sing to the LORD! Let us shout joyfully to the Rock of our salvation. ²Let us come before His presence with thanksgiving; Let us shout joyfully to Him with psalms. ³For the LORD is the great God, And the great King above all gods. ⁴In His hand are the deep places of the earth; The heights of the hills are His also. ⁵The sea is His, for He made it; And His hands formed the dry land. ⁶Oh come, let us worship and bow down; Let us kneel before the LORD our Maker. ⁷For He is our God, And we are the people of His pasture, And the sheep of His hand. Today, if you will hear His voice: ⁸"Do not harden your hearts, as in the rebellion, As in the day of trial in the wilderness, ⁹When your fathers tested Me; They tried Me, though they saw My work. ¹⁰For forty years I was grieved with that generation, And said, 'It is a people who go astray in their hearts, And they do not know My ways.' ¹¹So I swore in My wrath, 'They shall not enter My rest.'"

Word Received April 24, 2002

The gates are open and my glory is coming through into the center of your being. Rejoice and be glad for my victory is upon you! I am transforming you from glory to glory, as my Spirit fills you afresh with my wonder and joy. Worship the Ancient of Days with everything that is in you! Be joined and surrendered to my love as I lift you up into the heavenly places where my light reigns supreme. These are the times of refreshment and renewal that are promised. I am joining you to one another with golden bonds that cannot be broken. My wisdom will flow through you as you follow the leading of my Spirit: for he is in charge of what is taking place. He is saturating you with the oil of gladness that overcomes every obstacle and hindrance. My Kingdom is building to a crescendo in your life as my presence surrounds you with everlasting peace. You are standing on the pinnacle of the rest of your life, and I am launching you into a future that will take your breath away. Signs and wonders will be occurring all around you, as my miracles are being seen and received by those who need them. Healing and restoration will become the common occurrence for those you intercede for on my behalf. Wait and watch with great anticipation for what I will be doing in your life and in those you bring to me in prayer! The wave of my Spirit is building and is about to break on to the earthly scene. It will carry peoples and nations into the new day that I have promised. You, too, will mount up with wings like eagles and soar into the dawn that is breaking for you. Always seek my face and the intimacy of my passion for you! Be enveloped with my grace and favor as we are joined together forever. You are part of a great movement of my truth that will never end. My triumph is assured!

Love,
JESUS

Psalm 96

[1]Oh, sing to the LORD a new song! Sing to the LORD, all the earth. [2]Sing to the LORD, bless His name; Proclaim the good news of His salvation from day to day. [3]Declare His glory among the nations, His wonders among all peoples. [4]For the LORD is great and greatly to be praised; He is to be feared above all gods. [5]For all the gods of the peoples are idols, But the LORD made the heavens. [6]Honor and

majesty are before Him; Strength and beauty are in His sanctuary. [7]Give to the LORD, O families of the peoples, Give to the LORD glory and strength. [8]Give to the LORD the glory due His name; Bring an offering, and come into His courts. [9]Oh, worship the LORD in the beauty of holiness! Tremble before Him, all the earth. [10]Say among the nations, "The LORD reigns; The world also is firmly established, It shall not be moved; He shall judge the peoples righteously." [11]Let the heavens rejoice, and let the earth be glad; Let the sea roar, and all its fullness; [12]Let the field be joyful, and all that is in it. Then all the trees of the woods will rejoice before the LORD. [13]For He is coming, for He is coming to judge the earth. He shall judge the world with righteousness, And the peoples with His truth.

Word Received April 25, 2002

The wind of my Spirit is carrying the fragrance of my love across the land. I am touching hearts with a fresh understanding of my intimacy. I am gathering my beloved into close knit expressions of myself. You will be catalysts bringing new life to those who have been deceived and wounded. I am showering down the miracles of healing and restoration on even the most isolated and disappointed. I am changing the atmosphere and the conditions that have been bad into something glorious and fulfilling. Even the worst can become the best as my hand touches it with my compassion. Listen to my Spirit as he brings out the depth of meaning in my words to you. He knows my heart and yours as well. There is nothing that is beyond his reach. Enter again into the holy convocation where my presence is being manifested in my goodness and mercy. Worship with a grateful heart and a joyful spirit! I am with you my wonders to perform so rest in me and allow me to carry you where I will. It is not your efforts that produce the fruit. It is my anointing that brings everything together in the harmony of my peace that rests upon you. Sow in love and watch the growth that takes place. I will open your eyes to see my Spirit at work in all the things that are happening in your life. I will take care of your needs according to my will and plan. Trust me in everything that concerns you! Pray without ceasing as my Spirit leads you! Open doors and future plans are all in my hands. March under the command of my Holy Spirit at all times for he is your very life's breath! I have targeted many things for you and in due time you will see them. Approach everything that I give you with a sincere and faithful heart for I will work it through for you! All that I have is yours for you are my beloved!

Love,

JESUS

Psalm 97:10-12

¹⁰You who love the LORD, hate evil! He preserves the souls of His saints; He delivers them out of the hand of the wicked. ¹¹Light is sown for the righteous, And gladness for the upright in heart. ¹²Rejoice in the LORD, you righteous, And give thanks at the remembrance of His holy name.

Word Received April 26, 2002

I will awaken the nations to the glory of my presence. I am reaching out to the four corners of the earth with the message of my hope and truth. There is no place or people where my call will not be heard. I am shattering the weapons of oppression as I have destroyed the works of the evil one. Wait and watch for what I am doing in your life as well! I have great and wonderful things coming your way carried on the wings of my eagles. I will prosper you in every way possible as I restore many things that have been taken from you. There is a new unity coming to my people, one of my making. Proceed in what I show you and leave the rest in my hands! You have crossed an invisible line that puts you in a fresh position of relationship with me. I am conquering the demons in your life and bringing you into a great and open place of my freedom. I am partnering you with many that I have chosen to be in the forefront of what is happening in these days. Everything will lead to the fulfillment of my purposes for your life. Even the strange and the confusing will play their part in everything that will be taking place. There is a vision that is coming that will expand your expectations for the future. It is time for you to take your rightful place in the Kingdom of my righteousness. It is a position of gifting and celebration, which I have established. Come now into the relationship of deeper intimacy with me as you worship in the sanctuaries I have prepared for you. They will be tabernacles set up by my Spirit along the path of your journey with me. Enter the flow of my Spirit as he carries you along to the ultimate destination of my glory! I am saturating your life with fresh oil from the heavenly lamp stands. You will reflect my light wherever you are in the outpouring of my mercy!

Love,
JESUS

Psalm 98

[1] Oh, sing to the LORD a new song! For He has done marvelous things; His right hand and His holy arm have gained Him the victory. [2] The LORD has made known His salvation; His righteousness He has revealed in the sight of the nations. [3] He has remembered His mercy and His faithfulness to the house of Israel; All the ends of the earth have seen the salvation of our God. [4] Shout joyfully to the LORD, all the earth; Break forth in song, rejoice, and sing praises. [5] Sing to the LORD with the harp, With the harp and the sound of a psalm, [6] With trumpets and the sound of a horn; Shout joyfully before the LORD, the King. [7] Let the sea roar, and all its fullness, The world and those who dwell in it; [8] Let the rivers clap their hands; Let the hills be joyful together before the LORD, [9] For He is coming to judge the earth. With righteousness He shall judge the world, And the peoples with equity.

Word Received April 27, 2002

I am awakening those who have fallen asleep and my Spirit is calling them to attention. I am placing a fresh desire in them for a greater intimacy with me. I am touching their hearts with a longing for the open fields of my Kingdom. I am drawing them from their frantic seeking for meaning through their own efforts and I am bringing them into my peace. It is something that is beyond your understanding yet it captures your heart. It calls you to the deeper things, to the hidden fountains that lie within the relationship I seek for you. It is found in the total abandonment to the true worship of the Ancient of Days. It comes as you are carried on the wind of my Spirit that lifts you higher and higher into my presence. The things of earth begin to fade as you behold my glory and enter into it. It all happens within the confines of my loving embrace. All you are and ever will be are measured by the surrender to my love for you. It is my doing from beginning to end as you explore what it means for me to be your friend. These experiences of personal encounter in the fellowship of believers will transform you according to my desires. There will be a fresh enthusiasm for what I bring to all your relationships and to all that concerns your life. Everything you do will flow from a new purpose for your existence. You will see yourself as I see you for I truly rejoice over you with singing as I watch over you with the Righteous Father. We acknowledge you as our own and we are releasing what we have been holding in trust for you. There is much to come even though there are momentary lapses in the process, which cause you some concern. I will bring you through to that great and open place where all things will begin to come together in perfect harmony. Rejoice in it!

Love,
JESUS

Psalm 100

¹Make a joyful shout to the LORD, all you lands! ²Serve the LORD with gladness; Come before His presence with singing. ³Know that the LORD, He is God; It is He who has made us, and not we ourselves; We are His people and the sheep of His pasture. ⁴Enter into His gates with thanksgiving, And into His courts with praise. Be thankful to Him, and bless His name. ⁵For the LORD is good; His mercy is everlasting, And His truth endures to all generations.

Word Received April 28, 2002

The fire of my Spirit is about fall burning up the chaff and igniting the sacrifice of your hearts. The sweet fragrance will lift up to the heavens pleasing the Heavenly Father from whom all blessings flow. His will is for your good and for the renewal of your minds. He will transform you by my Spirit making significant inroads into the enemy's camp. His purposes and ways are beyond understanding, yet he will reveal his plans at the proper time. He will guide you into the truth that will set you free to worship me. Enter into my presence and let my joy wash over you! All that I have for you will enhance my Kingdom in your sight. Look beyond the moment into the future that I have for you. There is a light dawning on the horizon that will be reflected in your inward parts, as my Spirit takes up residence there. You are holy as you are being drawn into the circle of my righteousness, which is being declared by my Word spoken over you. It is the message of salvation, which comes with the power to liberate you from all bondage and deceit. My people who are called by my Name will come into the land filled with my promise and hope. It is a position that I have purchased by my blood and is given by my favor alone. It is not by effort but by faith and trust in me that it becomes a reality. All that I have is yours to freely enjoy in the times of our intimacy together. As you are joined to me, you are bonded with those who have received what I am pouring out by my Spirit. There is a building of mutual trust as I remove the barriers of distrust that have been present. I am restoring the hearts and minds of all who are being touched by the bounty of my Spirit. It is a gift from the Ancient of Days who watches over you with a heart of compassion. Come and dance before me in joyful celebration!

Love,
JESUS

Romans 1:16-17

[16]*For I am not ashamed of the gospel of Christ, for it is the power of God to salvation for everyone who believes, for the Jew first and also for the Greek.* [17]*For in it the righteousness of God is revealed from faith to faith; as it is written, "The just shall live by faith."*

Word Received April 29, 2002

Strike while the iron is hot, move as the anointing is upon you! Charge forward under the command of my Holy Spirit! Take the high ground that I have liberated for you and proceed according to my plan! I have set much in place for you as you faithfully follow what I have given you. There will be much at stake in these last days as the lies of the enemy seek to keep many in bondage. Forge ahead in the truth that I am revealing to you taking hold of the things that I am unveiling to you! Set your mind and heart on the purposes of my Kingdom and allow my Spirit to bring everything else into perspective. I will prosper you in all your ways as a sign of my favor resting upon you. Do not become confused but know that I have accomplished everything for the working out of your salvation. I am expanding your possibilities and opening the doors of opportunity. I will lead you to them and guide you through them. Always return to the joy that I have placed in you. It is a spring bubbling up with healing and revival for your body, soul and spirit. Remember, that everything is in my hands and that you are under the watchful eye of your Heavenly Father! He holds you in great esteem as his beloved child. Wait and watch what he will be doing to bring everything together in perfect harmony! Worship him for he is worthy of all your praise! Lift up holy hands dedicated to his honor and his majesty. Continue to pray as my Spirit leads you for he is bringing about many miracles for those you place before me. Strongholds are being removed as you press on with me. It is time to reap the harvest and to enter into the celebration of what I am doing in this time. You have cast your bread upon the waters many, many times and now you are beginning to see the returns. It is all to the good!

Love,
JESUS

Psalm 101:6
6My eyes shall be on the faithful of the land, That they may dwell with me; He who walks in a perfect way, He shall serve me.

Word Received April 30, 2002

I have opened the door to the future and I will guide you through it, as you trust in me. I have placed your feet on the upward path to the destination I have chosen for you. Follow the leading of my Holy Spirit as he works out your salvation in joy and gladness. Everything I have intended for you is in place and is being put into effect. All things are in my hands and nothing will be forgotten. There is a harmony to what I am doing as my Kingdom comes in power and light. My truth sets you free to enjoy my presence with you forever. Worship is a privilege and necessity for you as our intimacy grows and prospers. I have rescued you from the darkness and placed you in the fulfilling experience of my Kingdom. I am gathering many to be joined with you in the celebration of our mutual satisfaction. All that I have is yours as an inheritance that I have purchased for you by my blood upon the cross and in the completion of my Resurrection. I am imparting my character to you so that my touch can be expanded to everyone who comes into your sphere of influence. I am gathering the tribes and peoples to come to my holy mountain where the fire of my presence is being manifested. They will come drawn by my love and the Righteous Father's goodness. The new sound from heaven is being released for all to hear and for all to be transformed in the twinkling of an eye. The trumpets will herald this and the drums will cause all to come to attention. Let my Holy Spirit have his way in all that is taking place! Do not quench his efforts on your behalf by pride or unbelief! Catch hold of his vision for you and let it dominate your mind and heart! What is coming is far greater than what is past. Signs and wonders, miracles and healings are being poured out all around you. It is time!

Love,
JESUS

Psalm 103

¹Bless the LORD, O my soul; And all that is within me, bless His holy name! ²Bless the LORD, O my soul, And forget not all His benefits: ³Who forgives all your iniquities, Who heals all your diseases, ⁴Who redeems your life from destruction, Who crowns you with lovingkindness and tender mercies, ⁵Who satisfies your mouth with good things, So that your youth is renewed like the eagle's. ⁶The LORD executes righteousness And justice for all who are oppressed. ⁷He made known His ways to Moses, His acts to the children of Israel. ⁸The LORD is merciful and gracious, Slow to anger, and abounding in mercy. ⁹He will not always strive with us, Nor will He keep His anger forever. ¹⁰He has not dealt with us according to our sins, Nor punished us according to our iniquities. ¹¹For as the heavens are high above the earth, So great is His mercy toward those who fear Him; ¹²As far as the east is from the west, So far has He removed our transgressions from us. ¹³As a father pities his children, So the LORD pities those who fear Him. ¹⁴For He knows our frame; He remembers that we are dust. ¹⁵As for man, his days are like grass; As a flower of the field, so he flourishes. ¹⁶For the wind passes over it, and it is gone, And its place remembers it no more. ¹⁷But the mercy of the LORD is from everlasting to everlasting On those who fear Him, And His righteousness to children's children, ¹⁸To such as keep His covenant, And to those who remember His commandments to do them. ¹⁹The LORD has established His throne in heaven, And His kingdom rules over all. ²⁰Bless the LORD, you His angels, Who excel in strength, who do His word, Heeding the voice of His word. ²¹Bless the LORD, all you His hosts, You ministers of His, who do His pleasure. ²²Bless the LORD, all His works, In all places of His dominion. Bless the LORD, O my soul!

Word Received May 1, 2002

It is a time of freedom as the fullness of my Holy Spirit is poured out in a mighty flood upon my people. Choose this day to follow his leading as he catches you up into the wonder of my glory! All that has gone before has prepared you to enter into what I am bringing into being in this time. I am making a way for you through the seeming confusion and the hidden places of your soul. What I have in store for you is far greater than you can imagine, so do not despise the small beginnings. Take each step that I give you for they will ultimately bring you to the final goal I have set for you. There are new things happening all the time and I am enabling you to take full advantage of them. Let go of what was so that you can fly with what will be. There are many occasions for you to see my truth fulfilled and the lies quenched as you move ahead with me. Enjoy the worship opportunities that I give you and let them carry you deeper into our relationship with each other. It is there that our intimacy is fully experienced and increased. Rejoice that you have come to see this hour that is coming upon the earth! My triumph will become self-evident as my Kingdom is revealed for all to see. You will be exposed to my sovereign will in ways that have never before been seen. My Kingdom rule comes in power and light to redeem the world from their destruction. I have set many things in motion in many places, which will ultimately come together in the final analysis. I have placed you in a strategic position to take full advantage of what is going to take place. I have set my remnant at the pinnacle of the exposure of what is happening. You are anointed to carry out my plans for the days ahead when the full shaking comes. Be aware of who you are for I have truly called you for such a time as this!

Love,
JESUS

Psalm 118:14-16
¹⁴The LORD is my strength and song, And He has become my salvation. ¹⁵The voice of rejoicing and salvation Is in the tents of the righteous; The right hand of the LORD does valiantly. ¹⁶The right hand of the LORD is exalted; The right hand of the LORD does valiantly.

Word Received May 2, 2002

The fire of my truth will penetrate every heart and make a resting place for my love. I will set each one free who receives the outpouring of my Spirit. I will raise up a mighty people who will carry out my will and purposes. My anointing will empower them to do great deeds in my Name. I have overcome the works of the evil one and I am giving into your hands the keys of my Kingdom. You will open the gates of liberty for all to come into my holy presence. My inspiration will flood your souls with a hope and expectation that cannot be quenched. Follow the leading of my Spirit and do not rely so much on your own understanding! I am about to bring you into a wholly new way of seeing and knowing what I am revealing to you. It will be necessary for this time when many things out of the ordinary will be occurring on the earth. You will be carried by the wind of my Spirit as it blows with an even greater intensity in your life. Apart from me you will be helpless but with me you will accomplish great and wonderful things that I have set for you. Always carry the torch of my Spirit to light your way wherever you go! You will always be under my command and at my call. You are entering a door of transition that will bring you into a new place and position with me. It will be my doing that brings you there. Trust my wisdom and my love to sustain you in everything that will be taking place! Take one step at a time and do not look too far ahead for things will be changing very rapidly as you travel along the path I have for you. Continue to worship the Ancient of Days with an open and willing heart! Allow my Spirit to take you higher and deeper into the experience of our majesty. We are giving you an impartation of great value as you are joined to us there. Many will be coming with you!

Love,
JESUS

Psalm 105:1-4

[1]Oh, give thanks to the LORD! Call upon His name; Make known His deeds among the peoples! [2]Sing to Him, sing psalms to Him; Talk of all His wondrous works! [3]Glory in His holy name; Let the hearts of those rejoice who seek the LORD! [4]Seek the LORD and His strength; Seek His face evermore!

Word Received May 3, 2002

The light of my presence will flash across the heavens like a meteor and impact the hearts and minds of those who see it. I will explode in your midst transforming all with my power and love. None will be able to resist what I will be doing in their lives. Even the doubters will have to come to terms with what will be happening. My truth will prevail, as everything else will have to bow before it. Minds and hearts will be captivated by my mercy and compassion. There will be a willing surrender and yielding by all who receive it. Events and times will be subject to radical change as my Holy Spirit plants his banner among you. It will breed an attitude and expression of worship never before seen on the earth. You will enter into a holy convocation with the Ancient of Days that will last into eternity. You will honor him with a true sacrifice of praise and joy. The trumpets will speak the sound of my voice into the hearts and lives of those who have discovered a newfound trust in me. You will hear the clash of swords as I topple the strongholds of deceit around you. A sudden terror will come upon the enemy as I pursue him to his final destination. Meanwhile the rejoicing of the saints will flood the air with shouts and exclamations of wonder and thanksgiving. You will join in the festivities, as you have been faithful through the times of preparation. My anointing has sustained you through all the days of your life and it will continue to do so. You will be part of the triumphal vanguard that moves before me across the face of the earth. I have set you in place for this time and I will show you the part that you will play in it. I am gathering you together with those I have set apart for my Kingdom and its glory. You will carry the banners of my righteousness and victory. Just receive it!

Love,
JESUS

Romans 5:1-5

¹Therefore, having been justified by faith, we have peace with God through our Lord Jesus Christ, ²through whom also we have access by faith into this grace in which we stand, and rejoice in hope of the glory of God. ³And not only that, but we also glory in tribulations, knowing that tribulation produces perseverance; ⁴and perseverance, character; and character, hope. ⁵Now hope does not disappoint, because the love of God has been poured out in our hearts by the Holy Spirit who was given to us.

Word Received May 4, 2002

The dawn is breaking and the new day has arrived. The trumpets will sound to announce the outpouring that I have promised. My grace and favor is sufficient for all your needs and it is freely given for all to receive. My river of life is coming to flood tide and it is about to burst over the conventional banks. Nothing can contain it or hinder it. The river keeps moving as it carries everything with it. Even the most resistant will have to let go and go with the flow. There are spectacular events ahead of you as the tide has turned for the good. Hope is rising up within you to a magnitude never before experienced in your life. Rest in my love and in the assurance of it for all the days of your life! Come and worship at the feet of the Ancient of Days and allow his blessing to fill you with great joy. All that is coming has been prophesied from the beginning only it's understanding has been hidden for a time. Take your place in what is happening and no longer deny the destiny I have for you! There are many doors being opened for you and they all lead to the same outcome the fulfillment of your calling in me. There is a fresh anointing for this time, which will overcome every obstacle and propel you forward into the mighty deeds I have planned for you. The wind of my Spirit will be at your back lifting you to greater heights than you ever thought possible. My concerns are for you and for those you lift before me in prayer. The gates have been flung open for my glory to come in and cover you with the gifts of my Kingdom. Proceed along the path that my Spirit is leading you! It will take you to the mountaintops where my eagles soar in the light of my presence. You will behold our majesty as it is portrayed to you in the fullness of time. Come away with me my beloved into my embrace!

Love,
JESUS

Isaiah 6:1-8

¹In the year that King Uzziah died, I saw the Lord sitting on a throne, high and lifted up, and the train of His robe filled the temple. ²Above it stood seraphim; each one had six wings: with two he covered his face, with two he covered his feet, and with two he flew. ³And one cried to another and said: "Holy, holy, holy is the LORD of hosts; The whole earth is full of His glory!" ⁴And the posts of the door were shaken by the voice of him who cried out, and the house was filled with smoke. ⁵So I said: "Woe is me, for I am undone! Because I am a man of unclean lips, And I dwell in the midst of a people of unclean lips; For my eyes have seen the King, The LORD of hosts." ⁶Then one of the seraphim flew to me, having in his hand a live coal which he had taken with the tongs from the altar. ⁷And he touched my mouth with it, and said: "Behold, this has touched your lips; Your iniquity is taken away, And your sin purged." ⁸Also I heard the voice of the Lord, saying: "Whom shall I send, And who will go for Us?" Then I said, "Here am I! Send me."

Word Received May 5, 2002

I have opened the windows of heaven to pour down my blessings upon my people. I have broken through to the heart and I am transforming your lives in my righteousness. The light of my presence is released among you as the wonder of my glory surrounds you. The power of my Holy Spirit is being released to carry out the intended will of the Righteous Father. I am capturing you with my love and healing all your diseases. Flesh and blood cannot contain all that I am doing in this time. Set your focus on the things above and everything else will fall into place! My desire for you is to fully experience the freedom of my Spirit as he releases himself in the depths of your being. Proceed along the path that he has placed before you for it will bring you to the perfect outcome of your life! All things will work together for good as my image is deeply implanted in you. I direct the tides of time as they roll over the earth bringing to completion what the Heavenly Father has purposed. Wait with great anticipation for what I am unveiling upon the earth! The greater things that I have promised are beginning to take place among you. My Kingdom is being manifested in all its power and glory. Continually seek my face in worship and reflection in the renewing of your minds! I will change your thinking as I impart more and more of myself to you. There is an increase coming in all things for you. What is coming will be far greater than anything you have ever known. Yield your heart to mine in a deeper and more profound intimacy! Surrender up your sword that I might place in your hands the sword of my Spirit that has never failed. It produces radical results at every swing and the enemy is terrified of everyone who wields it. I am joining you together as a sanctuary of my Holy Spirit, ho!

Love,
JESUS

Ephesians 2:19-22

19Now, therefore, you are no longer strangers and foreigners, but fellow citizens with the saints and members of the household of God, 20having been built on the foundation of the apostles and prophets, Jesus Christ Himself being the chief cornerstone, 21in whom the whole building, being fitted together, grows into a holy temple in the Lord, 22in whom you also are being built together for a dwelling place of God in the Spirit.

Word Received May 6, 2002

My eagles are flying into the sunrise of my new day. You will see my light in the fullness of my glory. My truth is established in you and my purposes are going forward in the fulfillment of your destiny. You are my anointed one who carries my banner before me. Sights and sounds will carry the wonder of my Kingdom for all to perceive. You are approaching the goal that I have set before you and you are striking home my victory. Sincerely desire what I have for you and boldly grab a hold of it for this is the will of your Heavenly Father. I am ushering in a new era for my people as they come into their rightful position in me. You are chosen to do mighty deeds in my Name to honor the Father who loves you. You have become a dedicated follower and now I have placed you at the forefront of what I am doing. Faithfulness is the foremost imprint of my character upon you. Seek my face no matter what the circumstances for it is there that you will always find my peace! Worship the Ancient of Days in the integrity of your being for you truly are a holy one to me! I have sown the seed and I have watered it with my Spirit now comes the harvest. The wonder of my healing presence will go with you wherever you are for I have sent you there. Each day will be an open door for you to behold the working of our majesty with you. Trust me for I have everything in my hands and under my sovereign control! It will often be beyond your understanding for it comes from above where the throne of my grace reigns. Receive it with true gratitude and watch how I make everything come together in perfect harmony. There is much yet to come as you stand at the entrance of a whole new way of living in my Kingdom. The heavens declare my glory and my blessings will abound!

Love,
JESUS

Isaiah 55:6-9

⁶Seek the LORD while He may be found, Call upon Him while He is near. ⁷Let the wicked forsake his way, And the unrighteous man his thoughts; Let him return to the LORD, And He will have mercy on him; And to our God, For He will abundantly pardon. ⁸"For My thoughts are not your thoughts, Nor are your ways My ways," says the LORD. ⁹"For as the heavens are higher than the earth, So are My ways higher than your ways, And My thoughts than your thoughts.

Word Received May 7, 2002 – Aalborg, Denmark

My eagles have landed and everything is well in hand. I am fulfilling my purposes even as I speak. My Word is my bond and I am working everything out as I have planned. I am finishing off all my preparations and you will see many things come into play for you. Watch with a fresh intensity as I parade all of what I have before you! There are many opportunities for you as I pour out my anointing upon you. Everything has its purpose in my Kingdom where I rule in the majesty of my presence. I am cooperating with you as you proceed along the path I have designed for you. I am building you together with many that I have called to rally around my banner of righteousness, which is planted in your heart by my Holy Spirit. Be aware that I am always near, my wonders to perform. The enemy cannot hold a candle to what I am doing on the earth. The light of my truth will burst forth with an explosive quality as it creates a whole new atmosphere for you to carry out your calling in me. Approach everything with great expectations for a revelation of what I am accomplishing with you! Get in line with my Holy Spirit as he leads you in the direction I have for you! Sow the seed knowing that it will produce a harvest far beyond anything you could imagine. What I have in store for you today will overwhelm you in great and marvelous ways. I am restoring what was taken from you and I am adding much more to it. All of it will bless you and all who will see it and receive it for themselves as well. Walk in my ways for they are far superior to anything else you might encounter. Do not become anxious about anything just trust my love for you! The wind of my Spirit is about to blow from a totally new quarter with an even greater power than you have ever seen. Let it catch you up in what I have for you!

Love,
JESUS

Romans 8:28

[28]*And we know that all things work together for good to those who love God, to those who are the called according to His purpose.*

Word Received May 9, 2002

I have found a way to retrieve all that was lost and to restore it to its rightful condition. I am truly working all things together to the good as my Holy Spirit takes hold of you. Be at peace in your present situation for I have everything under control! What the world sees is only a shadow of the true reality. I am making all things new and complete in my mercy. You are to go in and possess the land that I have liberated by my Resurrection victory! What the enemy meant for evil I will turn to a marvelous manifestation for my purposes. Proceed as my Spirit leads for he knows the outcome of every action! The trumpets will sound as the faithful gather to worship the Ancient of Days with a heartfelt enthusiasm. Receive and believe everything that I have promised you! Focus your attention on what I am declaring to you and follow it to the conclusion I have determined for it. My truth will prevail in every instance as you draw ever closer to me in our new found intimacy together. I am raising up a people who will do mighty deeds in my Name as they bow before me in a radical holiness. I am calling upon you to take your banner and follow after me! I have established you in my Kingdom, which cannot suffer defeat no matter what comes against it. You are standing on my holy mountain where the lighting of my presence flashes all around you. It is a time of great strength and power for you as you carry out my plans and purposes. There is much that is coming that will more than compensate for everything you had to endure in the past. I have placed in your hand and in your mouth the sword of my Spirit, which will vanquish all opposition to my revelation. My healing of hearts will carry great weight in the proclamation of my message to those you will encounter in the days ahead. Rejoice in all of it!

Love,
JESUS

Romans 8:37-39

[37] Yet in all these things we are more than conquerors through Him who loved us. [38] For I am persuaded that neither death nor life, nor angels nor principalities nor powers, nor things present nor things to come, [39] nor height nor depth, nor any other created thing, shall be able to separate us from the love of God which is in Christ Jesus our Lord.

Word Received May 14, 2002

I have opened the way for you as you travel in my Name. I have made many preparations for you and they are all coming into play in the days ahead of you. Do not become anxious over anything that is taking place for I am with you in all of it. The friends I have prepared for you will enrich your life in many and varied ways. Continue to seek my face in the light that I am revealing to you! Be patient with everyone and every thing that you will encounter as you proceed along your chosen path. Many miracles will be happening, some that you never even suspected would happen. Know that I have truly anointed you to take your place in the forefront of what will be going on in the unveiling of my plans. I have partnered you with many who are of a like mind and spirit, some who are not aware of it at this time. They will be awakened to it at the appropriate time. They will accept my challenge and they will come to the knowledge of the truth that I am declaring to them. Step aside when it is time to do so and allow my Holy Spirit to have full reign in their lives. Follow my lead at all times as my Spirit shows you the direction you must go! Take the occasions that are given you to bear witness to my presence in your life! Worship in your heart and then when possible in the gathering of my people for a renewal of your hope! I am sending you where you are going and I will determine the outcome of what will be taking place. Always be aware of your surroundings for I will be found there among them. Trust my wisdom in you for I am giving you the words of life to share with those who need to hear them. The wind of my Spirit is beginning to blow with a fresh intensity where you are and it will shake everyone around you. Get ready to receive all that I have for you and rejoice in it!

Love,
JESUS

Psalm 113

1Praise the LORD! Praise, O servants of the LORD, Praise the name of the LORD! 2Blessed be the name of the LORD From this time forth and forevermore! 3From the rising of the sun to its going down The LORD's name is to be praised. 4The LORD is high above all nations, His glory above the heavens. 5Who is like the LORD our God, Who dwells on high, ⁶Who humbles Himself to behold The things that are in the heavens and in the earth? ⁷He raises the poor out of the dust, And lifts the needy out of the ash heap, ⁸That He may seat him with princes—With the princes of His people. ⁹He grants the barren woman a home, Like a joyful mother of children. Praise the LORD!

Word Received May 18, 2002

I will fill your days with joy and gladness as you follow the direction I have planned for you. Do not fear the mountains or the floods for I have overcome them all with my righteousness! Move ahead in what I am revealing to you with a fresh boldness and confidence! I am partnering you with many that have heard and answered my call for these latter days of my Kingdom work. Proceed on the path that I have set before you and do not deviate from it! I have placed a mission deep in your heart that is unfolding as you journey on the way that is before you. I am gathering my people in power pockets where they will be able to carry out what I have projected for this time. Be ready to act as my Spirit leads you and do it with both courage and wisdom! You will see many hearts turned to me, which were not ready to receive until now. There will be a radical transformation in them far greater than anything you have ever seen. Follow the inspiration of my Spirit as he breaks new ground for you! You will not depart from what he has spoken into your heart even though you did not fully comprehend it. He will unveil it, as you need to understand it. I am increasing the depth of your desire to worship the Righteous Father which will be released as you meet together with those of like mind and spirit. There will be an explosion of my presence among you when heaven and earth will kiss in the embrace of a newfound intimacy with me. Be aware at all times of the destiny I have placed within you! I am following through on everything that I have intended for you. There is a moment of rest before the great outpouring of my Holy Spirit comes upon the earth. When it comes it will fill your life with a totally new dimension of my glory and purpose. Receive it all in gladness and joy!

Love,
JESUS

Psalm 117
¹Praise the LORD, all you Gentiles! Laud Him, all you peoples! ²For His merciful kindness is great toward us, And the truth of the LORD endures forever. Praise the LORD!

Word Received May 19, 2002

The winter is over and the spring has come as the light of my presence fills the horizon. No one sees it unless they look for it and no one finds it until they receive it. All that I have for you is a gift that I freely pour out on all peoples for it is the manifestation of my love that has no limits. Today my Spirit makes it real for you in ways you could never even imagine before this time. Continue to worship in my Spirit and to pray as he guides you for the doors are open to what I am doing among you! The hidden things are being revealed so you can apply the wisdom that I am unfolding in you. Be ready at all times to enter into the flow of my Spirit that is coming to you! Everything that I have for you is about to burst out before you as you proceed on the path I have laid out for you. Always be aware that you are not your own but my servant and my representative that I have sent to prepare the way of my coming! There are many who are being brought together to experience the fullness of my joy and hope. It is the encouragement that is needed to carry out the mission I have set before you. My truth will come like lightning flashing across the skies. It will strike the heart of even the most unbelieving soul. I am awakening those who have fallen asleep and I am opening their eyes to the reality of my majesty. They will react in totally new ways to what they will be seeing. They will shout and dance as they are filled with a fresh enthusiasm for my Kingdom. They will lift up the banners of my victory as they march forward to take charge of the land that I have liberated. Amazing things will be happening as more and more of the captives are set free. Healing miracles will be poured out as hungry hearts are turned toward me. All of this will be my doing as the wind of my Spirit is poured out!

Love,
JESUS

Psalm 118:13-16

[13]*You pushed me violently, that I might fall, But the LORD helped me.* [14]*The LORD is my strength and song, And He has become my salvation.* [15]*The voice of rejoicing and salvation Is in the tents of the righteous; The right hand of the LORD does valiantly.* [16]*The right hand of the LORD is exalted; The right hand of the LORD does valiantly.*

Word Received May 20, 2002

There is fire, fire as my Holy Spirit is poured out upon you! There is power, power as he breaks through to the hearts of all who receive him! I have come to bring life to your tired souls and to fill you with a fresh enthusiasm for my Kingdom. You have been waiting and praying for what I will do among you. Now it begins as the light of my new day dawns upon you. My call to worship the Righteous Father, the Ancient of Days is a call for release of my people to their rightful place in me. It is a time of joy as you enter into the freedom I have won for you in my Resurrection. Do not hide any longer but step forward on the world scene with the boldness and confidence that my Spirit gives you! The preparations have been made and now you are to walk in the power authority that I have given you. Speak with one voice as my Spirit directs you! He is the source of your harmony with one another. There is no one greater or lesser for you are one people in me. The anointing I give you is to fulfill the Father's will for this time. Seeds have been sown and the ground has been cultivated now is the harvest. Just words will no longer satisfy I am bringing an explosion of power that will transform lives in the blinking of an eye. Waves of my Spirit will begin to roll over the land until it is flooded with new life. Yes the hearts of the fathers will be turned to the children as the hearts of the children are turned to the fathers. There will no longer be separation or division but a unity of love never before seen on the earth. It will catch the attention of those who have not seen the truth and they will now embrace it with great fervor. You are standing within the gates of the New Jerusalem in the peace of the heavenly Kingdom! It is where my presence is manifested in all my glory and majesty!

Love,
JESUS

Isaiah 12

¹And in that day you will say: "O LORD, I will praise You; Though You were angry with me, Your anger is turned away, and You comfort me. ²Behold, God is my salvation, I will trust and not be afraid; "For YAH, the LORD, is my strength and song; He also has become my salvation."' ³Therefore with joy you will draw water From the wells of salvation. ⁴And in that day you will say: "Praise the LORD, call upon His name; Declare His deeds among the peoples, Make mention that His name is exalted. ⁵Sing to the LORD, For He has done excellent things; This is known in all the earth. ⁶Cry out and shout, O inhabitant of Zion, For great is the Holy One of Israel in your midst!"

Word Received May 22, 2002

Deep calls to deep as I pour out more of my Holy Spirit upon you. I am bringing a new day into play in every way. All that has happened before was only the introduction to even greater things for my people. You are moving in the flow of my river and it is increasing in intensity. You will be riding on the crest of the wave that will be carrying you along faster and further than you have ever been. My glory will be present as you worship and celebrate my goodness and mercy. Get ready to receive a double portion of my anointing which will prepare you for the larger mission I have in store for you! I am extending the vision I have for you far beyond the horizon that you can see with your natural eyes. Follow me into the place I have established for you and do not let the lies of the enemy deter you! He is under your feet for I have conquered him at the cross. Continue along the path that I have laid out for you and never look back! I am also adding many to my victory train from every direction imaginable. You are beginning to see the first fruits of a great harvest. Place your confidence in me and be bold in your efforts on my behalf for I have already made a way for you! You have already stepped across the dividing line that is your future. I will be turning many things around for you as I gather together the many who have been enlisted for my cause. Raise the banners and sound the trumpets as you move into the positions of authority that I have established for you! There will be a freshness in your words and manner as you take hold of what I have for you. The power of my presence will be with you as you speak as my chosen vessel for this time. The oil will flow down from my hands upon your head as you carry out my purposes. Get ready to herald in the majesty of my Kingdom among you!

Love,
JESUS

Romans 12:1-2

[1]I beseech you therefore, brethren, by the mercies of God, that you present your bodies a living sacrifice, holy, acceptable to God, which is your reasonable service. [2]And do not be conformed to this world, but be transformed by the renewing of your mind, that you may prove what is that good and acceptable and perfect will of God.

Word Received May 23, 2002

I have called you from the beginning to enter into the fulfillment of my purposes in this time. Be aware of my direction at all times for I am guiding you down to the smallest detail! I am setting many things in order according to the will of the Heavenly Father. He knows your heart and the desire for faithfulness to all that I give you. I will always show you the way to go even on the cloudiest day. My light will always break through and show you the path you should take. There are many coming to join you in the things I have prepared for you to do. It will sometimes seem overwhelming to you but be of good cheer for I am in command. Hear my voice wherever you are and whatever the circumstances for I am continuously speaking to your heart! Keep the focus that I give you and follow through with what I show you! Worship from the depths of your being as my Spirit plunges into your innermost places of intimacy! He binds us together with the Righteous Father with bonds of love that can never be broken. You have a future and destiny that will be accomplished as I direct you to it. Always be open to the changing direction of the wind of my Spirit! Do not hold on to what no longer serves my plans for there is so much more to come! Be willing to let go at anytime I tell you and do not look back! What was may be interesting but it may have no significance for this time. Sometimes you may need to burn some bridges so you are not tempted to go back when things may become very challenging for you. Always remember that I am with you and my Holy Spirit has taken charge of your life! The new ways will always be better than the old for they will have my fresh anointing upon them. Rest in the assurance that I am working everything out to my perfection! Always walk in the freedom of my Spirit!

Love,
JESUS

Luke 8:15

[15]*But the ones that fell on the good ground are those who, having heard the word with a noble and good heart, keep it and bear fruit with patience.*

Word Received May 24, 2002

I have won the victory again in your lives as my Spirit has taken new ground in your existence. My plans are going forward as you rest in me and you trust in what I am doing with you. There are many open doors for you and there will always be enough time to complete what I have for you. Waiting and watching in prayer is one of the most effective tools you have in my Kingdom. Alongside of it is your dedicated worship of the Ancient of Days. These two will accomplish the will of the Heavenly Father in your lives. They are channels for my Holy Spirit to release his power and life in you. You will see the miracles and signs and wonders that have been promised. They will confirm the words I have put in your mouth that are the sword of my Spirit! Be ready at all times to move and act as my Spirit leads you for he has the authority to fulfill the will of the Father through you. My presence in you is touching those around you with my love and my mercy. I am setting the captives free so they can fully enter into the wonder of my Kingdom. I will show you great and marvelous things as you continue on the road I have set before you. Each day will be complete in itself as I carry out my purposes in it. Follow the direction of my Spirit at all times even in the ordinary details of your life. Approach everything with an expectant heart and a willing spirit! The wind of my Spirit is picking up intensity as it comes from a new direction never before experienced. It is changing the formation of things to conform more closely to the will of the Righteous Father. The old wineskins have burst and the new ones are being filled. It is my new day that is dawning for my people and it will bring a total transformation of everything you know. You have sown my seed now enter into the joy of my harvest!

Love,
JESUS

Psalm 126

¹When the LORD brought back the captivity of Zion, We were like those who dream. ²Then our mouth was filled with laughter, And our tongue with singing. Then they said among the nations, "The LORD has done great things for them." ³The LORD has done great things for us, And we are glad. ⁴Bring back our captivity, O LORD, As the streams in the South. ⁵Those who sow in tears Shall reap in joy. ⁶He who continually goes forth weeping, Bearing seed for sowing, Shall doubtless come again with rejoicing, Bringing his sheaves with him.

Word Received May 25, 2002

I have increased your anointing for what is yet to come. I am fulfilling your calling in every direction so that my deposit in you will be multiplied for others as well. Continue to be faithful to what I have put in you as you follow your destiny in me! There are even greater things yet to come as the circle of my compassionate connections are being completed. You are in the center of my will and the Heavenly Father does watch over you with singing. Proceed as my Spirit gives you the direction for each day! Sometimes the trumpets will sound as you go forth in triumph, while at other times it will be a still soft voice that you hear. Always be open to the opportunities that I present to you and grab a hold of them with boldness! I am partnering you with many that have been transfixed by the light of my glory. Be prepared at all times to bear witness to what I have given you as well as declaring the fresh Word from heaven! Everything works together for good to those who love me and follow after me. I will show you the eagles and doves that minister in my Name. They carry the message of my truth in power and gentleness. You will always find your place with them for you carry their inherent qualities as well. Enter into the flow of my Spirit as you worship from a heart filled with fervent devotion to my Kingdom. I will encompass you around with a shield of hope and faith that the enemy cannot penetrate. He will always flee from you, as you stand firm in your convictions. The new wave of my Spirit is about to break on the shores of your life. It will carry you further than you have ever been in your life. Take no thought for tomorrow for each day's glory is sufficient in itself! The time is coming when my people will worship together on my holy mountain. It will be a time of great joy for all!

Love,
JESUS

Romans 15:13
[13]*Now may the God of hope fill you with all joy and peace in believing, that you may abound in hope by the power of the Holy Spirit.*

Word Received May 29, 2002

I have finished the race and the victory is won, so I pass it on to you. Follow in my footsteps as I lead you on in triumph! Walk in the power of my love as you approach the opportunities I place in your path! Trust my will for you and allow it to have its perfect work in you! There is much more coming as you walk in my Spirit all the way. What you have seen is only the beginning of a great and powerful out pouring of my glory and majesty. Keep your focus on what I reveal to you and hold it as a treasure that we share with one another. Too often in the past you spoke before the time I have set to release what I have shown to you. Take some time to reflect before you share so that it will fully clear to you. There is time enough for everything that I have planned for you. Cross over to the other side now and turn in another direction that I will give to you. I am gathering many who have been waiting for the right moment and place that I have for them. You will see many crowding into the holy sanctuary that I have been building in secret. It will be seen in the true worship of those who have answered my call in the very depth of their being. I have sown my seed in them and it has been good ground that will produce much fruit that will continue to mature. Your place is also established there and it will continue to grow in the manifestation of my Holy Spirit through you. Fix your heart and mind on the things of my Kingdom for there you will find true joy and peace! The trumpets will sound and the people of my pasture will come together in a powerful move of my Spirit. They will wield the sword and the plowshare for both are necessary in what I am doing. You are partners with me in all that I have prepared for this time. Enter into it with a profound humility and a great expectation!

Love,
JESUS

Psalm 130

¹Out of the depths I have cried to You, O LORD; ²Lord, hear my voice! Let Your ears be attentive To the voice of my supplications. ³If You, LORD, should mark iniquities, O Lord, who could stand? ⁴But there is forgiveness with You, That You may be feared. ⁵I wait for the LORD, my soul waits, And in His word I do hope. ⁶My soul waits for the Lord More than those who watch for the morning—Yes, more than those who watch for the morning. ⁷O Israel, hope in the LORD; For with the LORD there is mercy, And with Him is abundant redemption. ⁸And He shall redeem Israel From all his iniquities.

Word Received June 4, 2002

I am following through with everything that I have begun with you. My fulfillment of visions and dreams are drawing near as you draw ever closer to me. It is your intimacy with me that I desire for you are my beloved. Open your arms and receive all that I hold dear for you. Occasions of trouble may appear but I have overcome them all as I use them for my purposes. Proceed along the path that I have chosen for you and do not turn back. Let go of what was in order to appropriate what will be. Follow the leading of my Holy Spirit as he cares for you and has your best interests at heart! Types and shadows will flow from my Word to give you insights into what is taking place. However trust only the revelation that I give you and discard the rest! I have established you in a partnership of mutual respect and support that will carry out my plans in these times. You will sometimes be walking a fine line as you thread through the circumstances that you will be facing. Still step out with boldness under the anointing I have placed upon you. Many will be drawn to me because of it. You are a catalyst that will produce an explosion of power upon my people. Your worship will become an intense experience of my glory being released among you. It will go on and on for days as it carries your deeper and deeper into my Kingdom. Your values will be changed, as what you thought was from me fades before the light of my truth. I will reaffirm what was truly from me and add greater insight to it. I will broaden your vision to encompass all of reality. You will see more of my hand at work in many things both great and small. Rejoice in it and receive it with thanksgiving! Now grab a hold of my staff and scepter as you rule and reign with me in the beauty of my holiness. I have chosen you for this time!

Love,
JESUS

Jeremiah 29:11-13
[11]For I know the thoughts that I think toward you, says the LORD, thoughts of peace and not of evil, to give you a future and a hope. [12]Then you will call upon Me and go and pray to Me, and I will listen to you. [13]And you will seek Me and find Me, when you search for Me with all your heart.

Word Received June 5, 2002

I have opened the door that no one can or will shut. I am proceeding with my plans for you and they are all for a good purpose. What has been related to you about what has been taking place is only a tip of the iceberg. There is a great groundswell of my Spirit about to break through the surface to inundate everything around it. The influence of his power and strength are spreading far and wide. The pockets of glory are filling up and overflowing. All that has been going on is a small foretaste of the greater things that I have in store for you. There is an expansion going on which will soon include every part of humanity in it. The light of my truth will be a powerful beacon drawing the multitudes to me. Open heavens will pour down the blessings of healing and restoration far beyond number. Exclamations of praise will resound throughout the land as the reality of my presence is felt and experienced in the hearts and minds of people everywhere. All this is still only a preparation for what is coming. The majesty of the Ancient of Days will become evermore apparent as your worship increases in freedom and intensity. It will be my Spirit sweeping over you and rolling down like waves of living water across the dry land. Nothing will be able to contain it for it will burst through the walls and boundaries until all you can see is a flood plain of my mercy. Grace upon grace will come to your aid as you are rescued from the direst of circumstances. I am with you my wonders to perform. I am joining you together in the bonds of my love that cannot be broken. You will be coming into a deeper intimacy with me where words will sometimes seem unnecessary. You will know as I know for our hearts will be joined. It will be the work of my Spirit carrying out the will of our Heavenly Father.

Love,
JESUS

1 Corinthians 2:9-16
⁹But as it is written: "Eye has not seen, nor ear heard, Nor have entered into the heart of man The things which God has prepared for those who love Him." ¹⁰But God has revealed them to us through His Spirit. For the Spirit searches all things, yes, the deep things of God. ¹¹For what man knows the things of a man except the spirit of the man which is in him? Even so no one knows the things of God except the Spirit of God. ¹²Now we have received, not the spirit of the world, but the Spirit who is from God, that we might know the things that have been freely given to us by God. ¹³These things we also speak, not in words which man's wisdom teaches but which the Holy Spirit teaches, comparing spiritual things with spiritual. ¹⁴But the natural man does not receive the things of the Spirit of God, for they are foolishness to him; nor can he know them, because they are spiritually discerned. ¹⁵But he who is spiritual judges all things, yet he himself is rightly judged by no one. ¹⁶For "who has known the mind of the LORD that he may instruct Him?" But we have the mind of Christ.

Word Received June 6, 2002

The explosion is coming for all the combustibles are in place. Wait for it with a joyful expectancy! I will fulfill your dreams and imaginings far beyond anything you could ever have thought possible. The light of the new day is breaking on the horizon and the reality of it all is about to take place. Remain in an attitude of worship and restful anticipation! Deal with the tasks at hand with quiet competence and allow my Spirit to take care of everything else. Everything has been set in place and I am proceeding according to the plan of our Heavenly Father. You will soon catch glimpses of the glory that is about to burst forth on the earthly scene. As you worship together in the anointing of my Spirit you will be carried to the highest places where our majesty dwells. Your hearts will experience the intimacy of our Divine Providence as it enfolds you in a loving embrace. Watch for it to take place as you celebrate the wonder and joy of our presence with you! Follow the leading of my Holy Spirit as he carries you from day to day! We have a partnership formed in the heavens that is being unfolded upon the earth. Accept those I place in your path and let the relationships develop according to my direction for they all have a purpose in my scheme of things. I am building a strong and unified Body to carry out the mission of the Ancient of Days. I am filling it with power and might to set the captives free and declare liberty to all who have lost their way. The light of my truth will always prevail over the lies and schemes of the evil one. Those who have been deceived by him will come to the dawning of my revelation. There is fresh bread for all to eat and living water for all to drink and none will go away empty. Be open to what I will be showing you and receive it with gratitude and joy for it is time!

Love,
JESUS

Psalm 138

¹I will praise You with my whole heart; Before the gods I will sing praises to You. ²I will worship toward Your holy temple, And praise Your name For Your lovingkindness and Your truth; For You have magnified Your word above all Your name. ³In the day when I cried out, You answered me, And made me bold with strength in my soul. ⁴All the kings of the earth shall praise You, O LORD, When they hear the words of Your mouth. ⁵Yes, they shall sing of the ways of the LORD, For great is the glory of the LORD. ⁶Though the LORD is on high, Yet He regards the lowly; But the proud He knows from afar. ⁷Though I walk in the midst of trouble, You will revive me; You will stretch out Your hand Against the wrath of my enemies, And Your right hand will save me. ⁸The LORD will perfect that which concerns me; Your mercy, O LORD, endures forever; Do not forsake the works of Your hands.

Word Received June 7, 2002

Breakthrough, breakthrough is the name of the game! I am fulfilling my promises as I am releasing my power to accomplish the mighty works in my Name. The wind of my Spirit is carrying you along as it moves to the place of divine appointment. There is a meeting place where all the forces of my truth will converge at one focal point. It will result in a mighty explosion of my glory that will shower down blessings all around. My people who are called by my Name will raise up the banner of my Kingdom that will stand proud and strong. You will carry my victory song sung by myriads of voices across the length and breadth of the land. Look to the heavens where my light is dawning as the new day breaks through and the shadows flee away. I have chosen you to be joined together with a great cloud of witnesses for this time. The deposits of my Spirit that have been placed within you are now beginning to bear fruit. The fruit will increase and bear more fruit as others eat of it. You are about to enter into another totally new dimension of worship as you again seek my face with your whole heart. Many worshippers will come forth freely dancing in the sunshine of my grace. Your faithfulness will be rewarded by ever-greater opportunities to see my glory at work. The healing of souls will increase exponentially as my Spirit brings them into my presence. The power of my truth will transform the multitudes and bring them into my salvation. Even the nations who dwell in darkness will see my marvelous light and come into my freedom. It is a time of great transition as the meteor of my power strikes the earth. Your calling is for this time as I add to it those who have also heard my voice for themselves. You will be one among equals who have bowed their knee to me!

Love,
JESUS

Isaiah 61:10-11

I will greatly rejoice in the LORD, My soul shall be joyful in my God; For He has clothed me with the garments of salvation, He has covered me with the robe of righteousness, As a bridegroom decks himself with ornaments, And as a bride adorns herself with her jewels. ¹¹For as the earth brings forth its bud, As the garden causes the things that are sown in it to spring forth, So the Lord GOD will cause righteousness and praise to spring forth before all the nations.

Word Received June 8, 2002

I have broken through and there is more to come. The whole earth will be filled with my glory and all nations will bow down before me. The focus for these days is an increased intimacy for your worship and reflection in me. I will bring you deep into the inner sanctuary of my heart where my joy flows abundantly. You will experience a fellowship of followers who have been totally inundated by my love. I will bring a release of power by my Spirit only dreamed of but not yet known. I am breaking the bondages that the enemy has held on to for years. I am bringing you up out of the depths of despair into my marvelous light. My redemption is drawing near for many who have stood outside and only looked in for it is the time of jubilee. I am crossing traditional boundaries as if they never existed. The folly that has been practiced is about to be exposed an expunged. There will be a clean slate for me to write my fresh revelations of truth. I will show you great and wonderful things that will make your heart sing with the praises of the King of kings. The Ancient of Days will be honored and glorified, as the Righteous Father is unveiled to each one. What was will be no more and what is coming into being will be far greater than anything you could imagine. Rest in my peace as I prepare the way for you! I am gathering together those who are being made ready to receive what I am about to pour out on all flesh. My Holy Spirit has taken complete charge of your life and he will bring you to where the eagles dare to soar into the direct light of the new day. Be attentive to my Spirit in you as he leads and guides all that you do or say! You have been waiting for this time and now it has begun to be played out before you. You have been faithful in what has been given now receive the rest!

Love,
JESUS

Joel 2:28-32

[28]*"And it shall come to pass afterward That I will pour out My Spirit on all flesh; Your sons and your daughters shall prophesy, Your old men shall dream dreams, Your young men shall see visions.* [29]*And also on My menservants and on My maidservants I will pour out My Spirit in those days.* [30]*"And I will show wonders in the heavens and in the earth: Blood and fire and pillars of smoke.* [31]*The sun shall be turned into darkness, And the moon into blood, Before the coming of the great and awesome day of the LORD.* [32]*And it shall come to pass That whoever calls on the name of the LORD Shall be saved. For in Mount Zion and in Jerusalem there shall be deliverance, As the LORD has said, Among the remnant whom the LORD calls.*

Word Received June 9, 2002

Seek my face and enter into my fond embrace as I carry you into my heavenly places! I seek your heart with mine as I restore your soul. I am finishing the work that I had begun even before you were aware of me. I have been leading you on to the destiny the Heavenly Father has been holding for you. My Holy Spirit is about to release a fire in your heart that will ignite mighty things on my behalf. There is an encircling of arms as I draw my people together in a deep inner joining of compassion and love. I am building a whole new structure of faith and inspiration. New wineskins are being formed as the old ones are being discarded for they have served their purpose. I am doing all things new so look forward to what is coming into being! Stir up the expectations that I have placed within you! Look with anticipation to what lies ahead of you! The walls are porous and they are about to collapse of their own accord. Come and worship with a fresh enthusiasm for my Kingdom, which is being revealed among you! Shouts of joy and praise are what reaches my ears and pleases my heart. Let the trumpets sound and the banners wave as you dance with all that is in you. I rejoice over you as you gather on my holy mountain where my Spirit holds court. Listen for his voice within you as his presence surrounds you. He will lift you up and direct your steps. Rely on his wisdom alone for he has the mind of the Righteous Father! My eagles are gathering and soaring around the place where heaven and earth kiss. The heavens are open to you and the wind of my Spirit is blowing free. It will carry you to uttermost parts of the universe and back again. It is beyond your understanding for it is an experience of our majesty, which is beyond mind and reason. Let it happen as my Spirit catches you up in it!

Love,
JESUS

Isaiah 25:6-9

⁶And in this mountain The LORD of hosts will make for all people A feast of choice pieces, A feast of wines on the lees, Of fat things full of marrow, Of well-refined wines on the lees. ⁷And He will destroy on this mountain The surface of the covering cast over all people, And the veil that is spread over all nations. ⁸He will swallow up death forever, And the Lord GOD will wipe away tears from all faces; The rebuke of His people He will take away from all the earth; For the LORD has spoken. ⁹And it will be said in that day: "Behold, this is our God; We have waited for Him, and He will save us. This is the LORD; We have waited for Him; We will be glad and rejoice in His salvation."

Word Received June 10, 2002

My flame is lit and my power is released for it is the time of my visitation. I will show you great and wonderful things in the days ahead. Trust my wisdom as you go through your day for my Spirit is guiding you! Choose this day those things that I point out to you and let the rest go for another day. There is much coming into your life as you wait upon me with an expectant heart. Proceed as my Spirit directs you for he has the whole plan before him! Your future in me is very bright and many things will begin to fall into place. I am bonding you closer with those who have yielded themselves to me for they are part of your destiny. Continue to seek my face in worship and contemplation for there is the intimacy that I desire to have with you! Flow in my Spirit for there will be a harmony in all that will be taking place. Come apart with me on a regular basis so we can compare notes and I can renew your strength in me! There is a growing joy that will find ever-greater expression in your life. Allow me the freedom to do with you what I will and to move you as I desire. I will open the doors before you and I will show you the steps to take as you go through them. Always depend on me for all your needs for I am your source and provision. Be careful about distractions for they can slow you down even though they cannot stop what I am doing in your life. Each day is an opportunity to see what I am doing even in the smallest details that surround you. All of life is precious to me and has a holy dimension for it is all mine. Just as you are mine so all that pertains to you is my concern. Know without a doubt that you are in my Kingdom where I rule in love and real authority! This authority has been delegated to you where I have placed you and you are to exercise it under the command of my Holy Spirit!

Love,
JESUS

Matthew 28:18-20

18And Jesus came and spoke to them, saying, "All authority has been given to Me in heaven and on earth. 19Go therefore and make disciples of all the nations, baptizing them in the name of the Father and of the Son and of the Holy Spirit, 20teaching them to observe all things that I have commanded you; and lo, I am with you always, even to the end of the age." Amen.

Word Received, June 11, 2002

The road less traveled is open before you as it leads you on to the joys I have prepared for you. Walk by faith trusting my love toward you! I will show you great and mighty things of my Kingdom that have been stored up for this time. Follow my Spirit as he opens the doors before you and guides you through them! Continue to worship under his anointing as he draws you ever closer to the Ancient of Days! I am following through with the many things that I have already begun in your life. I will be bringing things to a crescendo of blessing and outpouring of my favor. You are approaching the time when your position in me will be fully revealed for those who need to see it. I have made plans that are nearing completion as you pursue my calling upon you. I am refreshing your hopes and dreams as they are coming into being one after another. My Kingdom will be manifested in all its glory in the lives of those who have given themselves over to me with a sincere heart. The most unlikely will become the most likely to succeed and proceed according to my will. Watch and wait as I unfold things before you! Take hold of what I present to you and run with it! You will mount up with wings like eagles and you will run and not be weary. It is time to take your rightful place in my scheme of things. The lies of the enemy have been defeated by my truth that proceeds from your mouth. The sword of my Spirit is yours to carry out the purposes of the Righteous Father. There is a growing multitude of believers who are being added to my cause. They are being drawn from every place imaginable. Welcome them with open arms as your newfound brothers and sisters! The days ahead are under the harmonious direction of my Holy Spirit. He is your commander in chief follow him gladly!

Love,
JESUS

Psalm 143:8-10

8Cause me to hear Your lovingkindness in the morning, For in You do I trust; Cause me to know the way in which I should walk, For I lift up my soul to You. 9Deliver me, O LORD, from my enemies; In You I take shelter. 10Teach me to do Your will, For You are my God; Your Spirit is good. Lead me in the land of uprightness

Word Received June 12, 2002

The fire of my righteousness is about to burst forth melting all the opposition to it. Be aware of what my Spirit is showing you for he will reveal the pitfalls before you come to them. His prayers in your mouth are major instruments for dealing with whatever comes your way so pray without ceasing. Follow his leading at all times for he will guide you to the perfect outcome! There will be much happening at once but his wisdom will sort it out for you. The challenges are always opportunities for my glory to be seen. I will take everything and make something of great value for you and for my Kingdom. Even small beginnings can blossom into something mighty in my hands. Continue to worship and seek my face as you have been doing! It is there that our intimacy is restored and deepened. Catch the flow of my river as it takes you further and further into the mysteries of my presence. I am building a whole new way of serving in my Kingdom. I am unveiling it step by step until it is complete. Your place in it is assured, as you are faithful in those things that I have already given to you. The distractions will continue to fade away in the light of my coming day. Trust my judgment in all things even in the smallest of decisions since some of the major events depend upon them sometimes! The wind of my Spirit is again blowing from a new quarter as my Kingdom moves ahead in the will of the Righteous Father. Always be open to the change of direction as my Spirit directs you! There are many streams beginning to flow into my river so be alert to those who are joining with you. I will affirm and confirm those who are to be of particular interest for you. You have been prepared for such a time as this so do not be surprised at what will be taking place. Enter into my joy with great enthusiasm!

Love,
JESUS

Psalm 144

¹*Blessed be the LORD my Rock, Who trains my hands for war, And my fingers for battle—²My lovingkindness and my fortress, My high tower and my deliverer, My shield and the One in whom I take refuge, Who subdues my people under me. ³LORD, what is man, that You take knowledge of him? Or the son of man, that You are mindful of him? ⁴Man is like a breath; His days are like a passing shadow. ⁵Bow down Your heavens, O LORD, and come down; Touch the mountains, and they shall smoke. ⁶Flash forth lightning and scatter them; Shoot out Your arrows and destroy them. ⁷Stretch out Your hand from above; Rescue me and deliver me out of great waters, From the hand of*

foreigners, [8]Whose mouth speaks lying words, And whose right hand is a right hand of falsehood. [9]I will sing a new song to You, O God; On a harp of ten strings I will sing praises to You, [10]The One who gives salvation to kings, Who delivers David His servant From the deadly sword. [11]Rescue me and deliver me from the hand of foreigners, Whose mouth speaks lying words, And whose right hand is a right hand of falsehood—[12]That our sons may be as plants grown up in their youth; That our daughters may be as pillars, Sculptured in palace style; [13]That our barns may be full, Supplying all kinds of produce; That our sheep may bring forth thousands And ten thousands in our fields; [14]That our oxen may be well laden; That there be no breaking in or going out; That there be no outcry in our streets. [15]Happy are the people who are in such a state; Happy are the people whose God is the LORD!

Word Received June 13, 2002

I will lead you on to victory as you follow after me and trust in my wisdom! I will show you great and marvelous things in the most unusual and unexpected places. My plans for you are going forward as you rely on my strength to carry you. It is my joy to bless and magnify your life. Trust in my goodness toward you! There will be many open doors along the way as you continue in your journey with me. True life is filled with real expectations of my mercy being fulfilled in you. My love surrounds you at all times and I will never leave you no matter what the circumstances you may be facing. Beyond the shadows that you may sometimes encounter is my presence watching over you. Again and again the light of my countenance will come shining through to you. I have created you to be a light bearer as well as you reveal my truth to those who stand ready to receive. My will and work are daily being accomplished in your life. The wind of my Spirit will sweep you up into the higher places where my glory dwells in all its fullness. Your worship will be transformed there into something far more intimate and significant than you ever thought possible. You will experience visions and the power of my Spirit in all its majesty. Healings will be poured out drawing people into my fond embrace.

My love will become so apparent that no one will be able to resist it. I will have my way as I restore hearts, souls and minds. You will be amazed at what will be taking place all around you. My Kingdom will be manifested in everything that will be happening. Many things will come together in my perfect order, which will often be beyond your comprehension. I will be gathering together the elect who have heard my call to take the positions I am providing for them. Hear what my Spirit is saying to you!

Love,
JESUS

Psalm 145

[1]I will extol You, my God, O King; And I will bless Your name forever and ever. [2]Every day I will bless You, And I will praise Your name forever and ever. [3]Great is the LORD, and greatly to be praised; And His greatness is unsearchable. [4]One generation shall praise Your works to another, And shall declare Your mighty acts. [5]I will meditate on the glorious splendor of Your majesty, And on Your wondrous works. [6]Men shall speak of the might of Your awesome acts, And I will declare Your greatness. [7]They shall utter the memory of Your great goodness, And shall sing of Your righteousness. [8]The LORD is gracious and full of compassion, Slow to anger and great in mercy. [9]The LORD is good to all, And His tender mercies are over all His works. [10]All Your works shall praise You, O LORD, And Your saints shall bless You. [11]They shall speak of the glory of Your kingdom, And talk of Your power, [12]To make known to the sons of men His mighty acts, And the glorious majesty of His kingdom. [13]Your kingdom is an everlasting kingdom, And Your dominion endures throughout all generations. [14]The LORD upholds all who fall, And raises up all who are bowed down. [15]The eyes of all look expectantly to You, And You give them their food in due season. [16]You open Your hand And satisfy the desire of every living thing. [17]The LORD is righteous in all His ways, Gracious in all His works. [18]The LORD is near to all who call upon Him, To all who call upon Him in truth. [19]He will fulfill the desire of those who fear Him; He also will hear their cry and save them. [20]The LORD preserves all who love Him, But all the wicked He will destroy. [21]My mouth shall speak the praise of the LORD, And all flesh shall bless His holy name Forever and ever.

Word Received June 14, 2002

I will open the sluice gates of heaven and flood the land with my glory. My presence will fill all my believers with renewed strength and hope. I am restoring what was taken from you and adding much to it. I am turning even the worst circumstances around to accomplish my purposes. I am fulfilling dreams and visions and opening new ones to you. The time of my appearing is not far off, yet there is much to be done before it takes place. My truth is going out to every corner of the earth and my freedom is being released in every nation. This is the time to enter into worship with ever increasing diligence and commitment. It is there that I am able to impact my people with ever-greater deposits of my Spirit. Come with an openness and deep expectation at what I will be doing with you there! It is at that point that you will encounter me above the mercy seat where I dwell with the cherubim. Cast your cares upon me like bread upon the waters and I will return to you a hundredfold blessing. It is time for you to enjoy the returns of your faithfulness as you continue in your journey with me. You will mount up with wings like the eagles you are. You will soar into the high places where you will see beyond the mountains that surround you. What lies ahead will be even more majestic than what you have already experienced. The flow of my Spirit will carry you beyond the reaches of any limitations that have been put upon you. He will open great vistas of my goodness and my mercy to you. You will enter into my Kingdom plans with ever increasing enthusiasm and enjoyment. Worship with a sincere heart the Ancient of Days who watches over you with singing and rejoicing! Enfold yourself in his fond embrace and feel his anointing upon you. There is a fresh release of my power and light in you.

Love,
JESUS

Isaiah 25:1

¹O LORD, You are my God. I will exalt You, I will praise Your name, For You have done wonderful things; Your counsels of old are faithfulness and truth.

Word Received June 15, 2002

The way of the righteous shines brighter and brighter every day. I am unfolding before you my plans for your future filled with great and outstanding things. I will provide and provision you with every spiritual gift to carry out your mission here. Keep your focus on me as you worship and serve in my glorious Kingdom! My peace I give you as you follow in my triumphal train. You are marching under the banner of my Holy Spirit who commands in my Name. There is far more ahead of you than there was behind you. The greater things of my calling will be revealed in the days ahead as you follow my leading in faithfulness and humility. Proceed in the direction that my Spirit shows you and trust his wisdom at all times! The eagles are gathering on my holy mountain waiting for the wind of my Spirit to carry them to new heights in me. I am charging you with fresh energy as I enlarge your spheres of influence in my Name. What has been spoken of in the secret councils of the heavenlies will come to pass. I will unveil it all before you by my Holy Spirit. Listen to what he is saying in your inward parts! I am saturating you with his anointing for this time and place. Be open to what he gives you and follow through as he directs you! Worship the King of kings and the Ancient of Days with an increased enthusiasm and dedication! There is so much more to come so do not settle for less but seek the more that I have for you! The partners are increasing in numbers and devotion as the time is ripe for what I have intended for this time. See with my eyes as you enter into these last days with a strong sense of my destiny for you! I have placed my hope and expectations in you to inspire you to the mighty works I have prepared for you to do. You will have a newfound joy as my day dawns upon you!

Love,
JESUS

Isaiah 62:2-3

²The Gentiles shall see your righteousness, And all kings your glory. You shall be called by a new name, Which the mouth of the LORD will name. ³You shall also be a crown of glory In the hand of the LORD, And a royal diadem In the hand of your God.

Word Received June 16, 2002

The light at the end of the tunnel is my glory being revealed! It is a time of great openness for you as my Holy Spirit is bringing great inspiration to you. His wind is fanning the fire in your heart to a great conflagration. Your worship of the Ancient of Days will rise to new heights in me. You will experience the intimacy of the heavenly throne room on a daily basis, as my presence will be a continual reality for you. I am releasing my anointing and power for a great out pouring of my Holy Spirit. My Kingdom within you is joining with my Kingdom among you to produce mighty works in my Name. The greater things that I have promised are now coming to fruition. Healed hearts and bodies will serve as a witness to my goodness and mercy. Proceed in the direction I am setting for you and do not look back! Draw closer to me and I will draw closer to you for I am building a stronger relationship between us! My love and character are being indelibly etched on your life. It is also the foundation for all the connections I am making between you and others for I am establishing a Kingdom of my beloved ones. The calling I have upon your heart is about to move into a totally new dimension of influence. Continue to listen for my voice within you as I speak to you through my Word of prophecy! I will confirm everything that I am showing to you so you cannot be mislead. Trust what you hear from me! I am targeting a greater audience with my truth than you realize and many will be coming into my Kingdom. Rejoice and be glad! Celebrate the majesty of our wonder with you! Take charge of what we give you and follow it all the way! There is much to come and you have just entered into the beginning phases. Sound the trumpets raise the banners as you dance joyfully before me!

Love,
JESUS

Isaiah 61:1-3
[1] *"The Spirit of the Lord GOD is upon Me, Because the LORD has anointed Me To preach good tidings to the poor; He has sent Me to heal the brokenhearted, To proclaim liberty to the captives, And the opening of the prison to those who are bound;* [2] *To proclaim the acceptable year of the LORD, And the day of vengeance of our God; To comfort all*

who mourn, ³To console those who mourn in Zion, To give them beauty for ashes, The oil of joy for mourning, The garment of praise for the spirit of heaviness; That they may be called trees of righteousness, The planting of the LORD, that He may be glorified."

Word Received June 17, 2002

The way is clear so you can see forever into my glory. I have placed you where I have called you for now. Your future is wide open in me for there is much yet to come. I will turn everything to my good as I proceed with my plans for you. There will be occasions when you will find a pause in the events and this is for your benefit as well. Take the moments I give you to encounter me at a deeper level than you have ever been. I will renew you there with a sense of peace and tranquility. It will happen just before you move into the new things I have prepared for you. You have sown much and you will reap even more. I am challenging many of the concepts people have had about me. I am lifting them up to a higher level of understanding of my love and mercy. I am destroying the yokes of bondage and the old molds of comprehension. It is a totally new thing that I am doing in the days ahead. Wait for my Holy Spirit to guide you in them! Do not leap to your own conclusions about them. I will show you great and marvelous things yet to come. I am digging new wells as well as restoring old ones. My water of revival is about to spring up in many places simultaneously. You will not need to travel far to find them. There is a fresh excitement building in my people for what I am about to do among you. It is the faithfulness of the many that is making this possible. They have remained steadfast in the direst circumstances. Now the rest will be joined with them to enter into what I have prepared for this time. All that was necessary was a small crack that could receive my seed. Come and worship the Ancient of Days with a new found joy and enthusiasm! Come before him singing, dancing and praising his Name! Let the new sound go forth fulfilling the hopes and desires of my people!

Love,
JESUS

Psalm 149

¹*Praise the LORD! Sing to the LORD a new song, And His praise in the assembly of saints. ²Let Israel rejoice in their Maker; Let the children of Zion be joyful in their King. ³Let them praise His name with the dance; Let them sing praises to Him with the timbrel and harp. ⁴For the LORD takes pleasure in His people; He will beautify the humble with salvation. ⁵Let the saints be joyful in glory; Let them sing aloud on their beds. ⁶Let the high praises of God be in their mouth, And a two-edged sword in their hand, ⁷To execute vengeance on the nations, And punishments on the peoples; ⁸To bind their kings with chains, And their nobles with fetters of iron; ⁹To execute on them the written judgment—This honor have all His saints. Praise the LORD!*

Word Received June 18, 2002

I will follow through with what I have begun in you. Your destiny is mine and I have prepared it for you. I am breaking you away from many things that have hindered you in the past. It is a totally new day in me, which will result in many significant events for you. Approach everything with a sense of profound anticipation and expectation! I will be changing many things to more effectively carry out my purposes in the days ahead. Always be open to what I will be showing to you and be ready to take action as my Spirit guides you! At other times allow yourself to drift in my presence and to soak in my favor covering you. There is much that I have in store for you so do not discount anything that is happening. I am building to a crescendo the plans that I have made for you. Step into them with a passion for what I am doing and do not hold back from what is taking place. You will discover an even deeper level of worship as you release yourself more and more to the leading of my Holy Spirit. As you seek my face at every opportunity by yourself and with others you will find the revelation of the beauty of my holiness unveiled before you. The flow of my Spirit will carry you throughout the days and the nights. My presence will be your constant companion. I will send you partners of my choosing that will be of like mind and spirit . My vision is being accomplished through the working of my Spirit in all who call upon my Name. Sowing and reaping will be an ongoing task until everything has been accomplished to the satisfaction of the Righteous Father. Signs and wonders of healing and miracles will be on the increase. My Kingdom comes in power and light as my truth is proclaimed. Continue gathering together under the anointing of my Holy Spirit!

Love,

JESUS

Psalm 150

¹Praise the LORD! Praise God in His sanctuary; Praise Him in His mighty firmament! ²Praise Him for His mighty acts; Praise Him according to His excellent greatness! ³Praise Him with the sound of the trumpet; Praise Him with the lute and harp! ⁴Praise Him with the timbrel and dance; Praise Him with stringed instruments and flutes! ⁵Praise Him with loud cymbals; Praise Him with clashing cymbals! ⁶Let everything that has breath praise the LORD. Praise the LORD!

Word Received June 19, 2002

I have released my Holy Spirit in you to accomplish mighty deeds for my Kingdom. He is your companion and partner in all that is taking place. He restores the broken hearted and opens the prison doors. He brings my light into the darkness and turns night into day. Watch with him as he guides you along life's way! He will give you the wisdom to interpret what is taking place. Always follow his leading for he will show you the direction I have set before you! Rest in the confidence that he gives you and boldly speak as he gives you the words of life. What is about to happen will astound and amaze you but it is all my doing. Trust what I give you and act decisively on it! There is much that is coming and I have set many things up for you to walk in with joy and gladness. Continue to worship with enthusiasm as you enter into the holy of holies by my Spirit! He will bring you into the throne room where the Father and I reside. Sound the trumpets, beat the drums, and shake the tambourines as you dance before me in the freedom I have given you. Appreciate where you are in me and then look forward to where I am taking you for there is far more waiting for you. Search out those places where we can enjoy sweet communion together. They will be moments in time, which touch the hem of eternity. There will be individual contacts in the secret places entwined with gatherings of great wonder. It is my presence that will make it happen. I will take you there on the wings of the dove as you soar with the eagles far above the ordinary existence of every day. Time and place will not be the deciding factor; your heart turned toward me is what really matters. You will be experiencing new expressions of my glory as you are joined with those who have heard my call!

Love,
JESUS

Psalm 1:1-3

¹*Blessed is the man Who walks not in the counsel of the ungodly, Nor stands in the path of sinners, Nor sits in the seat of the scornful; ²But his delight is in the law of the LORD, And in His law he meditates day and night. ³He shall be like a tree Planted by the rivers of water, That brings forth its fruit in its season, Whose leaf also shall not wither; And whatever he does shall prosper.*

Word Received June 20, 2002

I will awaken my people to the future and hope that I am holding out to them. I will stir them up with my goodness and mercy. I am directing your steps so do not resist what I am showing you. Take prompt action as my Spirit guides you with his wisdom! Listen for my voice wherever you are for I am always with you! Move in the anointing I have given you and do not be distracted from it! My Kingdom is producing much fruit among you and many are coming to the knowledge of my truth. Nations are being impacted as my will is being done on the earth as it is in heaven. Cascades of my power are being poured out wherever my people are open to it. My Holy Spirit is taking you far beyond the ordinary as he carries out my work. You are established in a framework that I have prepared for you. Friendships and connections are all there to serve my purposes and to bless each one. I am calling upon you to take your position in the coming outpouring of my Holy Spirit. He is coming like a tidal wave to inundate the earth with my glory. Up until now you have been experiencing the ripples of what is coming. Wait with an expectant heart trusting that everything is in my hands! Proceed each day under the command of my Spirit who is my presence with you! Worship each day as if there were no tomorrow. Do not hold back anything from me. I will bridge any gaps that may appear. I am fulfilling my promises to you even those you are not aware of at this time. I am building up the partnerships that I have made for you as I am daily adding to them. My Kingdom is growing by leaps and bounds. You will see the reflection of this all around you as the multitudes come crowding into the places I have designated for them. Come and rejoice with me as these things are taking place!

Love,
JESUS

Isaiah 28:16
[16]*Therefore thus says the Lord GOD: "Behold, I lay in Zion a stone for a foundation, A tried stone, a precious cornerstone, a sure foundation; Whoever believes will not act hastily.*

Word Received June 21, 2002

The fire of the sword of my Spirit is about to penetrate deeper into your being. It will cauterize the old wounds and remove their scars. My Holy Spirit will set you free to become the one the Heavenly Father created you to be. Again do not despise the small beginnings for out of them great things will take place. Follow the leading of my Spirit at all times for he knows the goals that have been set for your life. He will reveal them on a need to know basis. Just continue to trust him and go in the direction he opens to you. Closed doors are not defeats they are only ways to the right doors I have for you. Place your hand in mine by faith and I will take you to the highest pinnacle of your life. I have already gone before you to prepare the places I have intended you to be. Neither turn to the right or the left until you hear my voice behind you guiding your steps. At times it may be full speed ahead and at others just rest where you are. Take each day as an opportunity for my grace and favor to work for you and for my purposes. Receive and believe all that I give you for you are the apple of my eye! You are presenting yourself approved in the anointing of my Holy Spirit. He has taken charge of your life and he is showing you the way to proceed. Be sensitive to what he gives you! I am removing the clutter so you can see clearly what I have for you. Continue to worship in my Spirit and truth for that is indeed the keys to my Kingdom! Enjoy my presence at all times for it surrounds you in the cloud of my glory! I will take you where no one has ever dared to venture. The power of my Spirit will flood through you as I open the gates of your life ever wider. There is a flow of my harmony and peace in all of it. Do not become anxious in the in between times for all of it is part of my plan. Rejoice instead!

Love,
JESUS

1 Corinthians 14:1-3

¹Pursue love, and desire spiritual gifts, but especially that you may prophesy. ²For he who speaks in a tongue does not speak to men but to God, for no one understands him; however, in the spirit he speaks mysteries. ³But he who prophesies speaks edification and exhortation and comfort to men.

Word Received June 22, 2002

I have opened the gates of my Kingdom wide to receive the multitudes that I am drawing to me. There is more going on than you can see for much has been hidden until the final hour. Move into the place I have determined for you and do not look back. There is so much ahead of you as my eagles begin their flight into the dawn of the day that is breaking. It is what I have prepared for this time. Seek my face in an attitude of true worship and devotion! I will meet you there in the intimacy of my love and acceptance. I will heal your wounds and cleanse all your diseases. I will restore your right mind and your true self. Always walk in the way of my Spirit for he is guiding you to my glory! His gifts are empowering you as his anointing rests upon you. You will speak with the authority I have placed upon you and your words will carry out what I have intended for them. They will never return to me empty for they are the will of the Righteous Father. This is a new time for you and there will be many changes coming as you follow me in my victory procession. The trumpets are sounding and the drums are carrying my message. Raise my banners and proceed into the fields that are white for harvest. I will be gathering my people from the places where they have been scattered. I will bring them from the darkness into my marvelous light. My truth will set them free to enjoy me forever. Nothing is wasted as my Kingdom goes forward in all its wonder. You are about to have the most unique experiences of my presence that have ever taken place on the earth. It is what I have been holding for these last days. Proceed as my Holy Spirit leads you for he will bring you to the greatest fulfillment of your life! Rejoice and be glad as everything comes together in my Name!

Love,

JESUS

1 Corinthians 15:20-25

[20]*But now Christ is risen from the dead, and has become the firstfruits of those who have fallen asleep.* [21]*For since by man came death, by Man also came the resurrection of the dead.* [22]*For as in Adam all die, even so in Christ all shall be made alive.* [23]*But each one in his own order: Christ the firstfruits, afterward those who are Christ's at His coming.* [24]*Then comes the end, when He delivers the kingdom to God the Father, when He puts an end to all rule and all authority and power.* [25]*For He must reign till He has put all enemies under His feet.*

Word Received June 23, 2002

Fire there is fire all around as my Holy Spirit explodes among you. There is a burning in your heart as his inspiration is ignited in you. My revelation is filling the air with joy and gladness. Shouts of praise are rising up in you as you experience a fresh outpouring of my anointing upon you. I am releasing my river of life and it will carry you deeper into my presence than you have ever been. Your worship of the Ancient of Days will be transformed as my love impacts you with a fresh fervor for my Kingdom. I am building to a crescendo of my power being released in you. The trumpets will blare and the drums will roll as my new sound is produced among you. It is my voice calling out to the hearts of people everywhere to come to me the savior of their souls. I will redeem them from their captivity and bring them into my glorious freedom. Healings will flow and lives will be completely turned around to me. My chosen ones will no longer be frozen in the lies of the evil one. I am restoring what has been lost and adding far more to it. It is a time of celebration as you experience all the wonders I have in store for you. I am bridging the gaps that have appeared in your lives and in your relationships. I am partnering you with those I am empowering for the working out of my Kingdom purposes. Lean into the wind of my Spirit and let it carry you to the heights that I have promised. You will soar among the eagles as they surround the heavenly throne where our majesty dwells. My Holy Spirit will transport you there as he releases you more and more from your earth bound existence. It is my victory that you will be experiencing in all the fullness of my glory. Yield yourself to my love and let it truly capture your entire being! This is my destiny for you!

Love,
JESUS

Isaiah 35

¹The wilderness and the wasteland shall be glad for them, And the desert shall rejoice and blossom as the rose; ²It shall blossom abundantly and rejoice, Even with joy and singing. The glory of Lebanon shall be given to it, The excellence of Carmel and Sharon. They shall see the glory of the LORD, The excellency of our God. ³Strengthen the

117

weak hands, And make firm the feeble knees. *4*Say to those who are fearful-hearted, "Be strong, do not fear! Behold, your God will come with vengeance, With the recompense of God; He will come and save you." *5*Then the eyes of the blind shall be opened, And the ears of the deaf shall be unstopped. *6*Then the lame shall leap like a deer, And the tongue of the dumb sing. For waters shall burst forth in the wilderness, And streams in the desert. *7*The parched ground shall become a pool, And the thirsty land springs of water; In the habitation of jackals, where each lay, There shall be grass with reeds and rushes. *8*A highway shall be there, and a road, And it shall be called the Highway of Holiness. The unclean shall not pass over it, But it shall be for others. Whoever walks the road, although a fool, Shall not go astray. *9*No lion shall be there, Nor shall any ravenous beast go up on it; It shall not be found there. But the redeemed shall walk there, *10*And the ransomed of the LORD shall return, And come to Zion with singing, With everlasting joy on their heads. They shall obtain joy and gladness, And sorrow and sighing shall flee away.

Word Received June 24, 2002

I have opened the portals of heaven to pour down my glory upon you. Bask in the sun of my righteousness and let it impact your whole being. I am restoring my tabernacle of worship in my own particular way. It is not made with hands but by my Spirit as it comes into being. It is established on surrendered hearts that are willing to lose themselves in me. Stand under the authority I am placing upon you and move only as my Holy Spirit directs you. Be still in the moments of deep intimacy with me and allow my love to rest totally upon you! It is there that new beginnings will occur. They are my doing from start to finish. Do not look around to see who is with you only focus on me as I release the deep springs of my grace within you. I am digging new wells as well as restoring some of the old ones. There is a moving and shaking going on as I put my plans in place. I am releasing a torrent of my Spirit that will wash away the last segments of the former ways. What is coming is a new creation of my making.

It will be so far beyond anything you have known that there will be no comparison. Look to me for all your needs for I will abundantly bless my people who are called by my Name! My healing power has been released among you and the signs and wonders are now appearing with greater intensity. They declare my Kingdom among you as I take my rightful place with you. Everything has a purpose in what I am doing. Enter the river as the level is rising. Abandon the shore for the very depths that are before you. Wind and rain will blow over you as my Spirit takes you further into the turbulence that is coming. Get ready to be swept off your feet by the revelation of our majesty. You will hear my voice like the sound of the trumpet calling deep within you. Respond from the depths of your being!

Love,
JESUS

John 7:37-39

37 On the last day, that great day of the feast, Jesus stood and cried out, saying, "If anyone thirsts, let him come to Me and drink. 38 He who believes in Me, as the Scripture has said, out of his heart will flow rivers of living water." 39 But this He spoke concerning the Spirit, whom those believing in Him would receive; for the Holy Spirit was not yet given, because Jesus was not yet glorified.

Word Received July 6, 2002

The fire of my Spirit is ready as the lightning of my righteousness is about to flash across the sky. I have already begun a new thing but many have been distracted by their own pursuits. Yet there is still time to enter into the festivities I have planned. It will not be like the world for mine go deeper with more lasting effects, some of them life changing. There will be an openness about what will be taking place so many can look in from the outside and may be intrigued by what is going on. If they watch it long enough they may be caught up in it. I will deal in a gentle manner with those who have not encountered me. Those who claim my Name without evidence will be dealt with more harshly. I am offended by lies and deceit. These are important times for my Kingdom as the purposes of the Righteous Father are being carried out. The wave of the future is now here. The preparations are complete and the trumpet is about to sound calling my people to a true solemn assembly. It is a gathering of those who have been fully sold out to the command of the Holy Spirit. It is an all or nothing condition. Follow your heart to the spiritual conclusion I have set for it! There is much more coming than you could ever suspect. The clouds are being moved aside so my glory can be seen. You will see it with the eyes of an eagle that can see into the very center without blinking. It is for the chosen that have been known by me from the beginning. I have held you in my hand and protected you from the evil one. There have been challenges and great pain for many of you but what is coming will far surpass all of it. Approach the new day with a great hope and expectation that is seated in me by faith! Worship the Ancient of Days with a joyful fervor and enthusiasm!

Love,
JESUS

John 12:44-46

[44]Then Jesus cried out and said, "He who believes in Me, believes not in Me but in Him who sent Me. [45]And he who sees Me sees Him who sent Me. [46]I have come as a light into the world, that whoever believes in Me should not abide in darkness.

Word Received July 9, 2002

The waiting is over and the festivities are about to begin. Holy Spirit revival is going to burst out all over the place. You have come through many troubles and now you will reap your rewards. You have been tested and proven faithful and you will see the fruits of your pain. Signs and wonders will appear as my Spirit takes hold of the reins and leads you into the tomorrow that I have promised you. Look forward with great expectation at what I will be doing among you. Many things will come together in many and varied ways. There will be prosperity in all areas of your life both spiritually and naturally. My wisdom will prevail at all times for I am fully in charge. Relinquish everything to me for I have it all already! Worship the Ancient of Days as though your life depended upon it for it does. In my presence is fullness of joy, healing and great satisfaction. I am declaring my will before men and all that I will be doing in the days ahead. I am pronouncing my authority on those I have designated for it. I will produce the fruits of repentance in all who will receive it. Those who walk away do so to their own destruction. This is the time of division between what is true and from me with what is the lie of the enemy. There is no longer any middle ground or permissiveness left. The time has grown suddenly short so what will be happening will be happening quickly. I have chosen whom I have chosen and it is for you to acknowledge it. The river of life is moving to floodtide and it will sweep everything before it. The gates of my Kingdom are wide open to receive everyone who will enter in. The trumpets will sound and the drums will beat. The banners will catch the wind of my Spirit and the dancing will reach a fever pitch. You will experience my glory in all its majesty so rejoice!

Love,
JESUS

Isaiah 48:10-11

[10]*Behold, I have refined you, but not as silver; I have tested you in the furnace of affliction.* [11]*For My own sake, for My own sake, I will do it; For how should My name be profaned? And I will not give My glory to another.*

Word Received July 10, 2002

I have opened the floodgates for my glory to come in and inundate you with my joy and gladness! Proceed along the road I have set before you for it is of my making. I will be a constant companion and reminder that it is my glory that will be seen in all that is taking place. Trust and follow my Holy Spirit as he leads you each day in all that you are doing! Indeed it is always my doing in and through you that is accomplishing every good work. My Spirit is producing fruit that will amaze and delight you. I am sowing and reaping all around you. There is no place that is not feeling the impact of my presence for I am taking visible charge of things as the time grows short. My Kingdom is being slowly unveiled as it has been growing among you below the surface of your lives. What has been hidden will suddenly come to light. Revelation knowledge will increase along side of the wisdom that goes with it. I will show you great and mighty things in the days ahead. Continue to bow down before me with sincerely humble hearts. Worship in the anointing of my Spirit as you experience my truth in your inward parts! You will catch a glimpse of the Ancient of Days high and lifted up before you. You will be drawn into his presence even to the third heaven where we rule in majesty and light. Our transforming power will encompass you and shield you. It will restore your bodies, souls and spirits. It is a new day for my people and some are yet to realize it but they will. My faithful ones are being accessed by my Spirit and are having their eyes opened to what I am doing. It is all my doing from beginning to end. I have promised that I would carry out the will of our Father and so I am. Prepare the trumpets to sound the call to my people! Raise the banners to greet my coming! It is time!

Love,
JESUS

Isaiah 50:4-5

"The Lord GOD has given Me The tongue of the learned, That I should know how to speak A word in season to him who is weary. He awakens Me morning by morning, He awakens My ear To hear as the learned. ⁵The Lord GOD has opened My ear; And I was not rebellious, Nor did I turn away.

Word Received July 11, 2002

The way is now clear for you to proceed in the direction I have planned for you. I will begin to open doors that were previously closed to you. There will be fresh incentives for what I will be bringing to you as you travel along the path I have set for you. The burdens have been taken from you and you are free to move as my Spirit leads you. He has your destination in sight and he will take you there when the time is proper for it. Now continue in what I give you daily to do and find the joy that I have for you there. The wind of my Spirit is about to sweep across the face of the earth disrupting the works of the flesh and the evil one. I am taking open charge of what is mine and I will do with it what I have determined to do. The changes that are coming are without precedent in their numbers and their magnitude. You are to continue in your worship as my Spirit directs you and to enjoy the fullness of my presence in it. The depth of our intimacy is increasing and is developing in many and varied ways. Our hearts are becoming more entwined as my will is being released more and more in your life. The sword of my Spirit is being honed and sharpened so it will be ready when the time comes for you use it under the anointing I have for you. My mission has truly become yours and I will unfold it before you. You have been faithful to me to the best of your ability and I will add much to you because of it. The triumph of my victory will be celebrated among you as a continuous feast as you see the restoration of my people. After having done all that you could, stand and see my glory pass before you. I will finish the good work that I had begun in you to my honor and praise. I will prosper all that you do in my Name as my Kingdom comes in all its light and truth. Embrace it with all your heart!

Love,
JESUS

John 17:13-19

[13]But now I come to You, and these things I speak in the world, that they may have My joy fulfilled in themselves. [14]I have given them Your word; and the world has hated them because they are not of the world, just as I am not of the world. [15]I do not pray that You should take them out of the world, but that You should keep them from the

evil one. ¹⁶They are not of the world, just as I am not of the world.
¹⁷Sanctify them by Your truth. Your word is truth. ¹⁸As You sent Me
into the world, I also have sent them into the world. ¹⁹And for their
sakes I sanctify Myself, that they also may be sanctified by the truth

.

Word Received July 12, 2002

Breakthrough time as the power of my Holy Spirit is being fully revealed to you. His presence in you is being stirred up to bring you to the place I want you to be in me. The forces of opposition are retreating before the onslaught of my worshipping believers. You have the enemy on the run as you worship the Ancient of Days with the fresh fervor I am putting in you. Lift up the banners of my victory and shout out my praises for I am with you! I am pleased with you and I rejoice over you. The light of my truth is ever expanding until the whole earth will be filled with my glory. The gates are open for the appointed to come in and enjoy the wonder of my Kingdom in all its beauty. I am changing hearts everywhere so they can enter in to what I have prepared for them. Continue to walk in obedience and faithfulness to what my Holy Spirit is showing you! He will take you places far beyond your greatest imaginings. He will catch you up in his wings and you will fly beyond the limits of your horizon. Deep calls to deep and you are one who has been touched by my hand for this time. Continue to be still before me and allow me to pour more of myself into you! I am forming a totally new body wineskin to receive the new wine that has been made ready for this time. It is filled with power and life transforming love. There will be healings as a sign of my love being manifested everywhere. I am removing the torment that has affected so many of my people. I am restoring more than a hundred fold what was taken from you and adding even more to it. Always follow the leading of my Spirit and speak only what he gives you. There are times to remain silent. Everything is in my hands and I am orchestrating what is taking place. Trust me and do not look so much at the circumstances for I have triumphed!

Love,
JESUS

Psalm 24

¹The earth is the LORD's, and all its fullness, The world and those who dwell therein. ²For He has founded it upon the seas, And established it upon the waters. ³Who may ascend into the hill of the LORD? Or who may stand in His holy place? ⁴He who has clean hands and a pure heart, Who has not lifted up his soul to an idol, Nor sworn deceitfully. ⁵He shall receive blessing from the LORD, And righteousness from the God of his salvation. ⁶This is Jacob, the generation of those who seek Him, Who seek Your face. Selah ⁷Lift up your heads, O you gates! And be lifted up, you everlasting doors! And the King of glory shall come in. ⁸Who is this King of glory? The LORD strong and mighty, The LORD mighty in battle. ⁹Lift up your heads, O you gates! Lift up, you everlasting doors! And the King of glory shall come in. ¹⁰Who is this King of glory? The LORD of hosts, He is the King of glory .Selah

Word Received July 13, 2002

The fire is coming to envelop my people in power and light. My truth will set you free to become what the Creator made you to be. I am restoring what the locusts have eaten and I am building a whole new life where my Holy Spirit dwells in all his glory. His rule and authority over you will produce mighty acts for the advancement of my Kingdom. Everything you do is totally dependent upon him for there is no room for margin or error. He alone carries you to where the Father wills you to be. It is his sovereign working in your life. Rest in this with confidence and rejoice that all that you are belongs to me! The depth of our intimacy is growing as each day more of my presence becomes released in you. Your worship is taking on new dimensions of clarity and creativity. Your heart is longing for more and more, which will be greatly satisfied. I am with you my wonders to perform and I am taking you forward into whole new realm of reality. You will experience the third heaven where I am along side of the Ancient of Days. You will see the crystal sea for yourself as my Spirit catches you up above the turmoil of this present time. Hear my voice deep within as I call out to you personally. I would speak to you and tell you of my love and compassion for you. I will stir up your passion for my Kingdom and the things eternal. I will bind up your wounds and seal the scars. All that I have for you is coming with an even greater manifestation of anything you have seen up until this time. You are resting on the wings of eagles that are lifting you up before my face. The solemn assemblies that I am calling into being will turn into great celebrations of my victory among you. I am binding you together with those I have brought alongside with ties that cannot be broken. Rejoice hilariously!

Love,
JESUS

Revelation 19:5-10

[5]Then a voice came from the throne, saying, "Praise our God, all you His servants and those who fear Him, both small and great!" [6]And I heard, as it were, the voice of a great multitude, as the sound of many waters and as the sound of mighty thunderings, saying, "Alleluia! For the Lord God Omnipotent reigns! [7]Let us be glad and rejoice and give Him glory, for the marriage of the Lamb has come, and His wife has made herself ready." [8]And to her it was granted to be arrayed in fine linen, clean and bright, for the fine linen is the righteous acts of the saints. [9]Then he said to me, "Write: 'Blessed are those who are called to the marriage supper of the Lamb!'" And he said to me, "These are the true sayings of God." [10]And I fell at his feet to worship him. But he said to me, "See that you do not do that! I am your fellow servant, and of your brethren who have the testimony of Jesus. Worship God! For the testimony of Jesus is the spirit of prophecy."

Word Received July 16, 2002

My light is dawning brighter and brighter every day. What I have planned is following along at a good pace. I am putting many things together simultaneously as I have much to do in these times. Be at peace and rest in my being with you in everything that is taking place! I am partnering you with many good people who have my Kingdom as their prime focus. I am building a great groundswell of believers who are carrying out mighty deeds in my Name. You will be amazed at what is yet to come. There are times when you will be set apart for my purposes and it does not reflect on you at all. I am producing a whole new way of looking at things for I am introducing some radical changes in the lives of those who follow me. What lies ahead of you is far greater than anything you have known up until this point in time. I am taking care of every detail for everything is of concern for me in the great scheme of things. I am pulling things together from far and varied situations. I am enhancing my messages to many people who are scattered across the world. No one place or nation has exclusive rights to what I am doing. I am drawing peoples into my Kingdom at a far greater rate than has ever been seen. I am reaching out to multitudes that have not been touched by my hope. I am restoring all that our righteous Father has given me. The nations are truly my inheritance. Continue in the flow of my Holy Spirit as he carries you along the road that I have established for you! Worship and glorify the Ancient of Days at every opportunity! Especially rejoice together as you gather before him in your praise and adoration of him! He is worthy of it all! Raise the banners in the wind of my Spirit as it begins to blow with ever-greater intensity! Let it carry you deeper into our presence!

Love,
JESUS

Psalm 28:6-9

6Blessed be the LORD, Because He has heard the voice of my supplications! 7The LORD is my strength and my shield; My heart trusted in Him, and I am helped; Therefore my heart greatly rejoices, And with my song I will praise Him. 8The LORD is their strength, And He is the saving refuge of His anointed. 9Save Your people, And bless Your inheritance; Shepherd them also, And bear them up forever.

Word Received July 17, 2002

I am opening the doors that I have promised and you are to step through them as my Spirit guides you. Follow his leading for everything that goes on in your life! He will always direct you correctly. Let go of any anxiousness for that is not productive for you. Instead step boldly into what I am unveiling to you. I will show you many things that will both amaze and please you. The sounds of fury will be replaced by a sweet sound that comes from heaven. It will speak even louder than anything else that has ever been heard. You will see many things come together as you proceed along the path that I have set before you. Trust my wisdom in every situation and look for it! The time of worship will become even more intimate as it grows in freedom under the watchful eye of my Holy Spirit. Cast your inhibitions aside and let me sweep you off your feet. There is a new song being released and a fresh anointing that comes with it. I am about to unveil some marvelous events that the Righteous Father has been holding in store for you. It is the reward for your faithfulness towards my Kingdom. My Spirit is about to release a power move for healing and restoration among my people. It will be a witness to my love and it will draw the multitudes to me when they begin to see it taking place. Keep your hearts humble and open to me and be willing to receive everything I have for you! The trumpets declare my glory with you and the shouts proclaim the wonder of my presence there too. Draw closer to me and I will draw closer to you. I am binding our hearts together so we can be one as the Father and I are one. The wind of my Spirit is increasing in intensity as he begins to move in a fresh way across the face of the earth. What you thought was impossible will now become possible!

Love,
JESUS

Psalm 29

¹Give unto the LORD, O you mighty ones, Give unto the LORD glory and strength. ²Give unto the LORD the glory due to His name; Worship the LORD in the beauty of holiness. ³The voice of the LORD is over the waters; The God of glory thunders; The LORD is over many waters. ⁴The voice of the LORD is powerful; The voice of the

LORD is full of majesty. ⁵The voice of the LORD breaks the cedars, Yes, the LORD splinters the cedars of Lebanon. ⁶He makes them also skip like a calf, Lebanon and Sirion like a young wild ox. ⁷The voice of the LORD divides the flames of fire. ⁸The voice of the LORD shakes the wilderness; The LORD shakes the Wilderness of Kadesh. ⁹The voice of the LORD makes the deer give birth, And strips the forests bare; And in His temple everyone says, "Glory!" ¹⁰The LORD sat enthroned at the Flood, And the LORD sits as King forever. ¹The LORD will give strength to His people; he LORD will bless His people with peace.

Word Received July 18, 2002

I am following through on everything I have promised. Watch and see what wonders I am performing on your part. Do not discount anything that I am showing you! Trust my love for you and do not lean on your perceptions alone! I am partnering you with those who will be long term companions on the journey I am opening before you. Rest in my compassion and wait on me for I am putting everything together for you! My timing is always perfect so do not run ahead of yourself. Waiting is trusting in my ability to do what I have intended to do. I have your best interests at heart and I am working accordingly even when you do not see it. In the meanwhile rejoice with me and worship with gladness and joy for this is the will of your Heavenly Father who loves you! You will move step by step into the future I have prepared for you. Each step will be significant in itself as you proceed along the path that is laid out for you. The wave of the future is my Holy Spirit carrying my people forward into the new day that is dawning on the earth. I am also enfolding you in my fond embrace which comforts and strengthens you to continue along your way. I will open the right doors when the time is ripe for now just rest in me. I am renewing you so you will mount up with wings like eagles so you can soar higher and further than you have ever been. There are no limits in my Kingdom for you can go on forever. In my economy nothing is wasted everything serves a purpose in bringing you to where

I want you to be. Do not despise the little things either for they all have a way of enhancing the life I am making for you. Always look up to me for I will direct your steps and show you what you need to know! I am gathering my flock and placing them in the pasture I have for them. You are my beloved and I am with you!

Love,

JESUS

Isaiah 55:8-11

[8] *"For My thoughts are not your thoughts, Nor are your ways My ways," says the LORD.* [9] *"For as the heavens are higher than the earth, So are My ways higher than your ways, And My thoughts than your thoughts.* [10] *"For as the rain comes down, and the snow from heaven, And do not return there, But water the earth, And make it bring forth and bud, That it may give seed to the sower And bread to the eater,* [11] *So shall My word be that goes forth from My mouth; It shall not return to Me void, But it shall accomplish what I please, And it shall prosper in the thing for which I sent it*

Word Received July 19, 2002

The Word of my Spirit will set you free as you receive it in your inward parts. Let it have its perfect work there and do not quench what I am speaking to you! Trust and rely on my wisdom rather than on your perception. What you see is not always what it seems. My discernment will open your eyes to see clearly what is taking place. Rely on me and not so much on your own understanding! Know that true wisdom is from above and it carries greater weight than anything you can find on the earth. I give it to many people sometimes they are not aware that it comes from me. It is time to catch the wind of my Spirit in the sails of your heart and be carried aloft into my presence. Worship the Ancient of Days with a fresh fervor and deep devotion! Enter into the flow of my river that comes down from the heavenly throne. Let it bring you where I have intended you to be. I will prosper you where you never thought possible as I open up things for you in the coming days. Seize the moments of opportunity that I give you! Do not let them weigh too heavily or too long on your mind! Move decisively as my Spirit directs you! I am about to open a whole panorama of opportunities and I will guide you to the right choices for you. Trust my love for you for I will always lead you in righteousness and truth! There are many changes coming and they will all be for the best so do not hold back from them! I am putting things in order for you and I am numbering your priorities. Come ever closer to me and I will share with you the deep things of my heart. There are greater things yet to come and I am working everything out everywhere. Rest in me as I give you those moments of quietness before me! There will be an ebb and flow to the working of my Spirit until the final outpouring. Enjoy it all!

Love,
JESUS

Ephesians 1:17-23

[17]that the God of our Lord Jesus Christ, the Father of glory, may give to you the spirit of wisdom and revelation in the knowledge of Him, [18]the eyes of your understanding being enlightened; that you may know what is the hope of His calling, what are the riches of the glory of His inheritance in the saints, [19]and what is the exceeding greatness of His power toward us who believe, according to the working of His mighty power [20]which He worked in Christ when He raised Him from the dead and seated Him at His right hand in the heavenly places, [21]far above all principality and power and might and dominion, and every name that is named, not only in this age but also in that which is to come. [22]And He put all things under His feet, and gave Him to be head over all things to the church, [23]which is His body, the fullness of Him who fills all in all.

Word Received, July 20, 2002

Blow the trumpet in Zion, sound the alarm for I am coming my will to make known! I am breaking off the dead branches so the rest will bear more fruit. I am turning the hearts of the children to their parents and the hearts of the parents to their children. I am restoring my Kingdom in all who will believe. My sovereign authority will rest upon you as you carry out what I have called you to do. It is in the heart alone that I take up residence for it is all a matter of my love being in you. Approach every moment with a sense of expectation about what I will be doing with you! My plans are going forward at a rapid pace and many things will be happening simultaneously. My righteousness and mercy are about to roll down upon you as I am the author of your salvation. I am drawing those who have not heard and I am awakening those who have fallen asleep. I am bringing all my sheep into the pastures that I have prepared for them. There will be one flock as the Righteous Father and I are one in unity and purpose. My day is dawning and nothing will be able to hinder it. Welcome it as you worship the Ancient of Days with a sincere heart joined to my Holy Spirit! It is in your dependence upon my Spirit for everything that my victory can be complete in you. I am deepening your relationship with me every day. I am drawing you into the heavenly councils where you can hear the voice of the Father in all its clarity. Listen and receive, hear and believe! I am expanding your tent further than you can see. Up until now your vision has been limited. Now I will draw back the curtain so you can catch a glimpse of what I have in store for you. My light and my truth will be your constant companions as you follow the path I have set before you. The wave of my Spirit is about to carry you to new heights in me!

Love,
JESUS

Ephesians 2:14-22

¹⁴For He Himself is our peace, who has made both one, and has broken down the middle wall of separation, ¹⁵having abolished in His flesh the enmity, that is, the law of commandments contained in ordinances, so as to create in Himself one new man from the two, thus making peace, ¹⁶and that He might reconcile them both to God in one body through the cross, thereby putting to death the enmity. ¹⁷And He came and preached peace to you who were afar off and to those who were near. ¹⁸For through Him we both have access by one Spirit to the Father. ¹⁹Now, therefore, you are no longer strangers and foreigners, but fellow citizens with the saints and members of the household of God, ²⁰having been built on the foundation of the apostles and prophets, Jesus Christ Himself being the chief cornerstone, ²¹in whom the whole building, being fitted together, grows into a holy temple in the Lord, [22]in whom you also are being built together for a dwelling place of God in the Spirit.

Word Received July 23, 2002

The lightning flashes and the thunder roars as my glory falls around you. Rise up my people and take charge of what I place in your hands! Be bold; be brave for I am with you my wonders to perform! I have washed you clean and I am strengthening you for what I have prepared for you. The way ahead is clear and my purposes are certain. Follow the leading that my Holy Spirit is giving you! Listen attentively as he speaks to you in your inward parts! Always keep your focus on worshipping in my presence and giving thanks to the Ancient of Days for his love and mercy! He watches over you and rejoices over your place in my Kingdom. Proceed as you are directed by my Spirit and wait when it is necessary to do so! You will never be late for what I have for you. I am the author of perfect timing and everything rests in my hands. There is much more coming for you and you will be amazed at what will be taking place. There is judgment and sorting out but I will do it! You are to enter into the flow of my river and let it carry you where I will. I have set you apart for my plans and I will see that they are accomplished. You have crossed the border into the land of my promise. I am widening the tent stakes on my sanctuary for the multitudes that I will be bringing there. It all rests with me, as you trust my wisdom and planning in your life. I have been with you from the beginning and I have been guiding your steps even though you were not aware of it. You are about to receive a whole new way of thinking and appreciating what I am doing in your life. The standards of the past are being revised upward until they conform to the vision of the New Jerusalem. My Kingdom rule is being continually manifested in your life as my Spirit is in command. Receive it all with a joyful heart!

Love,
JESUS

Psalm 34

[1]I will bless the LORD at all times; His praise shall continually be in my mouth. [2]My soul shall make its boast in the LORD; The humble shall hear of it and be glad. [3]Oh, magnify the LORD with me, And let us exalt His name together. [4]I sought the LORD, and He heard me, And delivered me from all my fears. [5]They looked to Him and were radiant, And their faces were not ashamed. [6]This poor man cried out, and the LORD heard him, And saved him out of all his troubles. [7]The angel of the LORD encamps all around those who fear Him, And delivers them. [8]Oh, taste and see that the LORD is good; Blessed is the man who trusts in Him! [9]Oh, fear the LORD, you His saints! There is no want to those who fear Him. [10]The young lions lack and suffer hunger; But those who seek the LORD shall not lack any good thing. [11]Come, you children, listen to me; I will teach you the fear of the LORD. [12]Who is the man who desires life, And loves many days, that he may see good? [13]Keep your tongue from evil, And your lips from speaking deceit. [14]Depart from evil and do good; Seek peace and pursue it. [15]The eyes of the LORD are on the righteous, And His ears are open to their cry. [16]The face of the LORD is against those who do evil, To cut off the remembrance of them from the earth. [17]The righteous cry out, and the LORD hears, And delivers them out of all their troubles. [18]The LORD is near to those who have a broken heart, And saves such as have a contrite spirit. [19]Many are the afflictions of the righteous, But the LORD delivers him out of them all. [20]He guards all his bones; Not one of them is broken. [21]Evil shall slay the wicked, And those who hate the righteous shall be condemned. [22]The LORD redeems the soul of His servants, And none of those who trust in Him shall be condemned.

Word Received August 1, 2002

The wind of my Spirit will come sweeping down the plain restoring health and prosperity to my people. It is time to see my glory in the land of the living as I carry out my purposes for those that I love. I am calling many who have not heard and awakening those who have fallen away. It is a time for coming together to worship the Ancient of Days and to acknowledge your allegiance to him. My Kingdom has come and is coming, as the gates are open to receive it. I have shattered the enemy and he is in disarray for his time grows short. Look to me for all your needs and trust that I will provide for them. The miracles, signs and wonders are going to appear with greater and greater intensity. Receive them for yourself as well and share them with those you meet along the way! Many will come to believe because of them. It will draw them into an intimacy with me that will enfold them in my hope and peace. I have called you to stand as a watchman upon the wall to declare the dawn of my new day. As you wait with me we are bonding together in ways you never thought possible. You are more than a servant in my house you are a close friend. What I am allowing in your life will increase your strength and faith in me. Our journey together has always been a personal one even when you did not notice me there. Soon it will be time to soar with my eagles as I am preparing you to join them. They will be gathering from the four corners of the earth to receive my commands for them. Then they will be sent out on my mission. You too will receive your orders as well when the time comes. Many things will be happening as you wait for I am building up my people to be a mighty force in the earth. Sound the trumpets, beat the drums and wave the banners as you welcome me among you!

Love,
JESUS

Psalm 42

[1]As the deer pants for the water brooks, So pants my soul for You, O God. [2]My soul thirsts for God, for the living God. When shall I come and appear before God? [3]My tears have been my food day and night, While they continually say to me, "Where is your God?" [4]When I remember these things, I pour out my soul within me. For I used to go with the multitude; I went with them to the house of God, With the voice of joy and praise, With a multitude that kept a pilgrim feast. [5]Why are you cast down, O my soul? And why are you disquieted within me? Hope in God, for I shall yet praise Him For the help of His countenance. [6]O my God, my soul is cast down within me; Therefore I will remember You from the land of the Jordan, And from the heights of Hermon, From the Hill Mizar. [7]Deep calls unto deep at the noise

of Your waterfalls; All Your waves and billows have gone over me.
⁸The LORD will command His lovingkindness in the daytime, And
in the night His song shall be with me—A prayer to the God of my
life. ⁹I will say to God my Rock, "Why have You forgotten me? Why
do I go mourning because of the oppression of the enemy?" ¹⁰As with
a breaking of my bones, My enemies reproach me, While they say to
me all day long, "Where is your God?" ¹¹Why are you cast down, O
my soul? And why are you disquieted within me? Hope in God; For I
shall yet praise Him, The help of my countenance and my God.

Word Received August 2, 2002

I am breaking through and releasing the fullness of my anointing upon you! I am healing and restoring my people to their rightful place in me. I am establishing my order in your lives and promoting you to the positions I have prepared for you. Open doors await you as you follow the leading of my Holy Spirit. He will show you the way through every dilemma and challenge. Proceed according to his direction at all times. Keep your focus on worship for this is how you love and honor the Ancient of Days according to his desires! Bowing down before him in an attitude of gratitude and thanksgiving pleases him greatly. Let my Spirit bring you to it for this is beyond your own capabilities. It is his working in your heart that produces it all. Rest in it and enjoy it as a gift of the Father's favor toward you! There are significant events beginning to appear on your horizon as you follow in my triumphant procession of believers. There is judgment for those who reject my call and it rests upon their heads alone. I am merciful and gracious for I will be patient with them yet there is a time when it will be called to task. The signs and wonders of my love are being poured out to bless and make whole those that they touch. I am changing the understanding of what I am revealing for many have missed what I have been speaking to them. I will show them clearly the meaning of my purposes and plans so they cannot be deceived. The enemy can no longer twist my truth for he will be fully exposed by it instead. The fresh wind of my Spirit has begun to blow across the nations and with it the unbelief is being replaced by a true trust in me. I will bind up the brokenhearted and place their feet on the upward way of my Kingdom. I am drawing you with them into the holy place where I reveal my majesty.

Love,
JESUS

Psalm 43

¹Vindicate me, O God, And plead my cause against an ungodly nation; Oh, deliver me from the deceitful and unjust man! ²For You are the God of my strength; Why do You cast me off? Why do I go mourning because of the oppression of the enemy? ³Oh, send out Your light and Your truth! Let them lead me; Let them bring me to Your holy hill And to Your tabernacle. ⁴Then I will go to the altar of God, To God my exceeding joy; And on the harp I will praise You, O God, my God. ⁵Why are you cast down, O my soul? And why are you disquieted within me? Hope in God; For I shall yet praise Him, The help of my countenance and my God.

Word Received August 3, 2002

The lightning of my truth will flash before your eyes as I fill you with a fresh hope for tomorrow. The way is clear for what I have planned for you so trust what I am showing you. I will bring you to a deeper level of intimacy with me through everything you will be experiencing. Let me sow into you more of myself as I take charge of the rest of your life. I will complete everything that I started and more. Follow the leading of my Holy Spirit as he gives you wisdom and insight for the days ahead! There are many open doors waiting for you, as the time is ripe for you to enter them. Until then continue as you have been doing worshipping the Ancient of Days with a fresh and inspired fervor. Enter into my presence with an expectant heart and a fresh knowing of who I am in your life! There is more coming as my people are being moved into the positions I have prepared for them. I am orchestrating the events and movements around you to serve my purposes. What you see is only part of what is taking place. There will be a time when what is hidden will be revealed for all to see. I am removing the barriers to the unity that I am bringing to my people. The lies of the enemy are being quickly exposed and remedied by my truth. The scattered bones are being linked together so my breath of life can be breathed into them. I am restoring those that I have called to enter into the fullness of my glory. Hear my voice as I personally speak to you my heart's concerns for you. Believe that I have your best as my personal desire! I am releasing my healing power in the land so that the miracles of my love can be received by all. It is time for the good news of my Kingdom to be revealed in signs and wonders. Catch the wind of my Spirit and go where it takes you for I am with you in it!

    Love,
JESUS

Colossians 1:9-14

[9]For this reason we also, since the day we heard it, do not cease to pray for you, and to ask that you may be filled with the knowledge of His will in all wisdom and spiritual understanding; [10]that you may walk worthy of the Lord, fully pleasing Him, being fruitful in every good work and increasing in the knowledge of God; [11]strengthened with all might, according to His glorious power, for all patience and longsuffering with joy; [12]giving thanks to the Father who has qualified us to be partakers of the inheritance of the saints in the light. [13]He has delivered us from the power of darkness and conveyed us into the kingdom of the Son of His love, [14]in whom we have redemption through His blood, the forgiveness of sins.

Word Received August 6, 2002

I am unveiling my plans as you go along. Do not get too far ahead of me just trust my discernment! I am walking you through what I have planned for you. The days ahead will be filled with my signs and wonders as the miracles begin to flow more freely. Be attentive to what

I am telling you in the quiet moments we have together! Sometimes in the busy times I will stop you to get your attention. Ahead of you lies a vast sea of possibilities and I will guide you in them. My purposes for you are being carried out by my grace and favor. You will receive what I have in store for you and you will have much joy with it. Continue to worship and bow down before the Ancient of Days for he is you true God and Lord! Enjoy our presence with you and let it swallow you up in the ecstasy of our love. We have been with you all along and we will see you through to the final fulfillment of all we have for you. Your partners will succeed with you in all that we have for them. There are open vistas being spread before you as you see our glory pass before you. You have come through some serious obstacles with flying colors and you will continue to do so. We are challenging the opposition at every turn and overcoming them with great power. There are more changes coming and they will all be good for you. Stand and watch with us as we bring everything into perspective for you! Always be open to what we show you and follow through what we show you! The wind of my Spirit is beginning blow afresh and he will be driving out the cobwebs that have collected over the years. Everything is coming together in perfect harmony for you. I am in charge and you are under the command of my Holy Spirit. The latter days of my house will be far greater than the former. Receive it all with thanksgiving!

Love,
JESUS

Psalm 47

¹Oh, clap your hands, all you peoples! Shout to God with the voice of triumph! ²For the LORD Most High is awesome; He is a great King over all the earth. ³He will subdue the peoples under us, And the nations under our feet. ⁴He will choose our inheritance for us, The excellence of Jacob whom He loves. Selah ⁵God has gone up with a shout, The LORD with the sound of a trumpet. ⁶Sing praises to God, sing praises! Sing praises to our King, sing praises! ⁷For God is the King of all the earth; Sing praises with understanding. ⁸God reigns over the nations; God sits on His holy throne. ⁹The princes of the people have gathered together, The people of the God of Abraham. For the shields of the earth belong to God; He is greatly exalted.

Word Received August 7, 2002

Keep your focus on me and do not lose sight of my promises! I am with you my wonders to perform and to carry out the perfect will of our Heavenly Father. Trust in me at all times and rely on what I am revealing to you! Always approach me with an open and expectant heart! I am bringing many things together as I have set in motion many things that the Righteous Father has given me to do. Your place in his plans is very important for he knows your heart and he rejoices over you with singing. Take one day at a time and do not reach beyond your grasp. Each step will lead you to the fulfillment I have for you. Rest in my peace and quiet your understanding for you are only seeing in part! There is so much more going on around you and much of it is hidden from your eyes. We are walking together as friends who trust and respect one another. Much has been sown and soon comes the harvest. Be attentive to what I am showing you for today! Continue in your worship of the Ancient of Days and bow down before him in humble surrender! Enjoy our majesty as it surrounds you with our glory. Let it lift you up into the heavenly places where you can see the crystal sea. There you will be refreshed and nourished to carry out the plans we have made for you. Disregard the circumstances and follow the leading of my Holy Spirit in you. He will confirm his words with actions that cannot be disputed. My healing and restoration are yours no matter what the conditions. The eyes of the blind will be opened when they see what I can do. Many will come to the truth as they are exposed to my miracles. They will be drawn into a personal encounter with me. Catch the wind of my Spirit as it begins to blow in earnest! Let it raise you up on eagle's wings into the dawn of the new day that is coming!

Love,
JESUS

Proverbs 3:5-6
5Trust in the LORD with all your heart, And lean not on your own understanding; 6In all your ways acknowledge Him, And He shall direct your paths.

Word Received August 8, 2002

The trials and tribulations are almost over as they have produced the fruit that matures. Your way is clear as you move beyond the present circumstances into a whole new world of possibilities. Nothing is too difficult for me as I am producing many blessings for all who call out my Name. Keep your focus on me and on what I am accomplishing in your life! Give respect to whom it is due and honor those who labor among you. Trust my direction for you and follow through with what my Holy Spirit presents to you! There is more to come than you could ever imagine. I will be opening doors that will seem amazing to you. I am proceeding with what the Righteous Father has planned for this time. Continue to worship with an ever-deeper commitment to the love we have for you! Let our presence encompass all that you are, filling you with the power and majesty of all that we are. My Spirit will lift you up to the high places where my eagles soar where you can behold the dawning of the new day that has been promised. I am turning everything to the good as you move in the direction that we have chosen for you. Take each day as an opportunity to see our glory manifested among you. Even the finest details can contain great miracles. Walk in the light, as I am in the light and you will see your deepest desires met. My truth is being revealed to the nations in many and varied ways for I am bringing things to their proposed conclusion. Multitudes upon multitudes will come flocking into my Kingdom as they see me for the first time. The enemy is being exposed for who he is and the eyes of many are being opened to the reality this brings. I am gathering together those who have been touched by my hand to receive a fresh anointing for the calling I have imparted to them. Rejoice!

Love,
JESUS

Colossians 3:13-17

¹³bearing with one another, and forgiving one another, if anyone has a complaint against another; even as Christ forgave you, so you also must do. ¹⁴But above all these things put on love, which is the bond of perfection. ¹⁵And let the peace of God rule in your hearts, to which also you were called in one body; and be thankful. ¹⁶Let the word of

Christ dwell in you richly in all wisdom, teaching and admonishing one another in psalms and hymns and spiritual songs, singing with grace in your hearts to the Lord. [17] And whatever you do in word or deed, do all in the name of the Lord Jesus, giving thanks to God the Father through Him.

Word Received August 9, 2002

I am bringing you through no matter what it looks like to the naked eye. I am working beneath the surface making the connections that need to be made. My ways are higher than your ways so trust my love and wisdom as I direct your steps. Take each day as I give it to you and know that I am accomplishing many things simultaneously. All I have for you is far greater than you can imagine at this time. My healing power is at work throughout the land and it comes in many and varied forms. I am penetrating deep within you and releasing my grace and favor there. Seeds that have been sown will now bear fruit as you proceed along the way that I have set before you. Catastrophic events will be occurring but they will not come near you. They too will be serving my purposes on the earth. Some things demand radical measures in order to correct them. I am establishing my people as a beacon light to draw the multitudes to me. You will be a lighthouse of hope revealing my truth for all to see. It is also time to worship me in the fullness of my Holy Spirit. Enter into the joy of our presence with you for that is your strength and sufficiency! Let my Spirit catch you up into the delight of our encounter with one another. Experience the fullness of our majesty with you. See the splendor of our glory being manifested among you. Seek out the gathering together of my faithful ones where we can have sweet communion together! Willingly yield to our will and purposes for you. We will bring you to a great and open place where our freedom can be known in all its wonder. Always seek my face with a tender and believing heart! What lies ahead of you will more than compensate for what was in the past. Move ahead with great expectations for what we will be doing in your life. Welcome it all gladly!

Love,
JESUS

Philippians 2:12-13
[12]*Therefore, my beloved, as you have always obeyed, not as in my presence only, but now much more in my absence, work out your own salvation with fear and trembling;* [13]*for it is God who works in you both to will and to do for His good pleasure.*

Word Received August 10, 2002

The fire of my Spirit is about to ignite a conflagration on the earth and you will be caught up in it. It will cleanse and purify as it empowers and transforms my people. It will release radical changes in the relationships and connections I am making among those I have called for this time. There will be a deepened awareness of my presence with you and a greater appreciation of what I am doing in these days. You will see with the eyes of the eagle into the dawning of the new day as it unfolds before you. There will be a shaking taking place as the false structures of man begin to crumble to make way for what I am building in the hearts and lives of those who have answered my call. The light of my truth will pierce the darkness of hypocrisy and deceit. The hidden things will stand naked before the eyes of my people. My ways will prevail as I lead you into the time and place I have prepared for you. Rest in my peace and give my Holy Spirit total right of way in your life! Truly let go of yourself into my hands for my purposes! I have a great future and hope for you, which will fill you with amazement. Trust me to take you there! You are about to enjoy a more profound intimacy in your worship of the Ancient of Days for this is the center of your relationship with me. It is there that everything begins and everything ends. It is the breath of life for you. I am also configuring you together with the others I have called into a panorama of gifts and dimensions of my glory never before seen on the earth. You will reflect my person for all to see and for all to desire for themselves. They will see my love and compassion revealed in you and through you. They will come seeking me because of it. It will be the start of the true revival not made with hands. Taste and see that it is good!

Love,
JESUS

Revelation 15:2-4

²*And I saw something like a sea of glass mingled with fire, and those who have the victory over the beast, over his image and over his mark and over the number of his name, standing on the sea of glass, having harps of God. ³They sing the song of Moses, the servant of God, and the song of the Lamb, saying: "Great and marvelous are Your works, Lord God Almighty! Just and true are Your ways, O King of the saints! ⁴Who shall not fear You, O Lord, and glorify Your name? For You alone are holy. For all nations shall come and worship before You, For Your judgments have been manifested."*

Word Received August 13, 2002

I have found a way for you that will lead far beyond the limitations of your expectations. It will be the fulfillment of all that the Ancient of Days has planned for you. It will be totally untouched by human hands or expectations. It will be all from us to you. Wait for the timing of it, as this is always crucial. Be open to what we give you in preparation for it. Everything that happens is for a purpose and in this case a very specific purpose of our making. Always remember my joy is your strength as I take you from glory to glory! Receive for yourself my robe of righteousness, as it will cover you from all harm and attack! Be resolved that you will follow me all the way through to the final outcome that is yours. No more detours or distractions but with your heart and soul fully fixed on me. My Holy Spirit has taken you in hand and he is leading you along the way that has been given to you. Stay in midstream where the flow is strongest and deepest as it carries you all the way. You have left the old things on the shore where they can no longer weigh you down. Continue to worship as you have been doing and allow my Spirit to show you even greater depths of intimacy with me! It is in my presence that you will find yourself healed and restored. Enjoy our friendship and let it lift you up in the challenging times. Proceed in those things I place before you and speak what I am revealing to you! The partners are all around you and they will hold up your arms when it is necessary. You are crossing over into a whole new way of living and with a radical understanding of what I am doing on the earth. There will be a flow and harmony to it, which will take you through the rest of your life and beyond. When the trumpet sounds and my call goes out the eagles will gather to await my orders. You will be among them!

Love,
JESUS

Psalm 103:1-5

¹Bless the LORD, O my soul; And all that is within me, bless His holy name! ²Bless the LORD, O my soul, And forget not all His benefits: ³Who forgives all your iniquities, Who heals all your diseases, ⁴Who redeems your life from destruction, Who crowns you with lovingkindness and tender mercies, ⁵Who satisfies your mouth with good things, So that your youth is renewed like the eagle's.

Word Received August 14, 2002

My Spirit is hovering over the chaos of life and bringing it all together according to the will of the Righteous Father. He is working in you and around you his wonders to perform. He is changing things in the blinking of an eye. He is moving mountains and opening the King's highway before you. Trust and rely on him completely and let go of what you think you see. Enter into the flow of my Holy Spirit for there is harmony and peace! Proceed as he directs you and wait for him to show you what it is! I am surrounding you by my grace and favor which will cover you all the days of your life. Listen for the rustling in the trees as the wind of my Spirit begins to blow. With it will come the latter rain to heal the parched earth. Be subject at all times to my desires for they carry your best at all times! Sometimes you have not realized that it has been my Holy Spirit who was leading you. It is his power that enables you to carry out my mission upon the earth. Especially when you worship the Ancient of Days his presence is with you lifting you up to new heights in me. We are in the process of washing and cleansing making our people whole again. Healing miracles are about to erupt on the earth as I am bringing everyone home to me. Place your own hands in mine and let me show you the wonderful things I have in store for you. Some things will remain hidden but I will let you see what will encourage you. Walk with your heads up, as my anointed ones for you are sons and daughters of my Kingdom. My Kingdom is the place of love; joy and peace so receive it gratefully! I am following through on everything I have promised. Wait for it with an open and expectant heart! I am reviving the hope that I have placed in you. The future is yours and I have provided for all of it. Now rejoice and be glad!

Love,
JESUS

Psalm 55:22
²²*Cast your burden on the LORD, And He shall sustain you; He shall never permit the righteous to be moved.*

Word Received August 17, 2002

The fire of my Spirit is falling, falling on the gatherings that I have assembled. It is the fire of edification and inspiration. It is the fire that burns up the false to be replaced by the pure. It is a fire that will sweep through the nations leaving no one untouched. It is the fire that I am releasing in you for healing and revelation wisdom for the days ahead. It is the fire that can transform in the blinking of an eye. You are about to be inundated by it as my Spirit again floods your life. He will catch you up beyond the imaginings of men into the holy atmosphere where we dwell in perfect harmony. You will experience what it truly means to be called by us, as you know us in a fresh and deeper way. As you enter in many will follow you there and others in turn will follow them and so my Kingdom will grow to its full capacity. The multitudes will be touched by what they see happening and they too will come flocking in as my Holy Spirit falls on them. You have been faithful with what I have given you, now be prepared for an even greater increase. Keep your eyes lifted up and focused on me! Continue to worship as your foremost vocation enjoying our presence and joy! I will open the curtain on what I have been doing in the lives of others that I have been touching to encourage you in your walk with me. More seed than you realize has been sown and greater and greater will the harvest be. Do not despise small beginnings for they are the time of building a sound foundation for what is coming! These days will be far more successfully evident than what went on before this time. Yet even in those times my glory has been revealed but now you will see an even greater manifestation. Come closer to me for I would speak my word into your ear for you alone to hear. My truth has set you free!

Love,
JESUS

1 Thessalonians 5:16-24

16Rejoice always, 17pray without ceasing, 18in everything give thanks; for this is the will of God in Christ Jesus for you. 19Do not quench the Spirit. 20Do not despise prophecies. 21Test all things; hold fast what is good. 22Abstain from every form of evil. 23Now may the God of peace Himself sanctify you completely; and may your whole spirit, soul, and body be preserved blameless at the coming of our Lord Jesus Christ. 24He who calls you is faithful, who also will do it.

Word Received August 20, 2002

You will always enter my gates with thanksgiving and come before me with praise for I have made your heart pure in me. Do not look back but look forward to what I am preparing for you there! The Ancient of Days is watching over you and he is rejoicing that you belong to him. Hear my voice and listen to what I am revealing to you personally and do not be distracted by what others may be saying. Approach me with an open heart and a willing spirit at all times. I have much to show you in the days ahead, which will totally change your way of thinking about many things. Do not be concerned about the others in your life for I am taking good care of them as well. Proceed in what I An showing you and allow my Holy Spirit to take you where I want you to go! Do not be overly concerned about the temporary lapses for some of them are built in for my purposes. The trumpets will sound when the time is ripe and they will come with a fresh sound from the heavenly throne room. It will energize my people with a new zeal governed by my wisdom and insight. They will know me in a greater and deeper intimacy than ever before. It is my desire for you to draw ever closer to me and find the reality of who I truly am for this is the center of eternal life. You are crossing a bridge that will disappear behind you for you cannot go back. There are many changes coming your way and all of them will be good but some of them will be challenging for you. Yet I am in the midst of them guiding your steps. Always trust in me and allow me to give you the dictates of your heart. Enter into your times of worship with a freshness and enthusiasm given by my Holy Spirit in you! He will always bring you alongside of me so I can touch the depth of your being again and again. Follow me without question or doubt!

Love,
JESUS

Jeremiah 9:23-24

23Thus says the LORD: "Let not the wise man glory in his wisdom, Let not the mighty man glory in his might, Nor let the rich man glory in his riches; 24But let him who glories glory in this, That he understands and knows Me, That I am the LORD, exercising lovingkindness, judgment, and righteousness in the earth. For in these I delight," says the LORD.